SARAH BROWN'S

Fresh Vegetarian Cookery

Over 200 exciting new recipes

Photographs by Philip Webb

BBC Books

To Paul, Ralph and Gregory

Published by BBC Books
an imprint of BBC Worldwide Publishing
BBC Worldwide Limited
Woodlands, 80 Wood Lane, London W12 0TT

First published 1995
© Sarah Elizabeth Brown Ltd 1995
The moral right of the author has been asserted

ISBN 0 563 37055 6

Designed by Tim Higgins
Illustrations by Chris Daunt
Photographs by Philip Webb
Styling by Jane McLeish
Home Economist Sarah Ramsbottom

Set in Linotype Sabon and Meridien Medium by
Phoenix Photosetting, Chatham, Kent
Printed by Cambus Litho Ltd, East Kilbride
Bound by Hunter and Foulis Ltd, Edinburgh
Colour separations by Radstock Reproductions Ltd, Midsomer Norton
Jacket printed by Lawrence Allen Ltd, Weston-super-Mare

Acknowledgements

I have had an enormous amount of encouragement and support whilst writing this book so it is hard to know where the thanks should begin.

However, first I would like to thank Ian Burleigh, Beverley Muir and Nick Cressey for working with me on the recipes: testing, tasting and making invaluable suggestions as well as being splendid company and not faltering at the endless washing up. My thanks too to Aruna Soujani for teaching me so much about her country's cuisine and for entertaining me with some wonderful days in her kitchen. I am also indebted to Vivian Martin, from *Vivian's*, Richmond, whose knowledge, and perhaps more important, love of good food has inspired me with many recipe ideas.

It was wonderful to have such a good team from the BBC. First my thanks to Heather Holden-Brown for her enthusiasm for this idea from the very outset, and her constant encouragement as the text began appearing. Thanks, too, to Anna Ottewill for overseeing the project in such a relaxed manner. I am also grateful to Susan Martineau for her excellent and thorough editing. My thanks to Frank Phillips for his thorough approach to the artwork, to Tim Higgins for his attractive and clear design, to Sarah Ramsbottom and Philip Webb for creating some mouthwatering photographs, and to Clay Perry for the cover photograph. I really felt everyone wanted to make this book as good as it possibly could be.

Writing a cookery book trespasses into all sorts of areas, from borrowing bits and pieces to loading friends down with emergency shopping. For all those useful contributions I must thank Elisabeth Brown, Anne May, Susan Birtwistle, Olivia Nuirrish and Jenny Littlejohns.

Last but definitely not least June McConnell who looks after Ralph and Gregory whilst I am working and who never seems to mind whether it is feast or famine. Tuesdays may never be the same again!

And finally, to Paul, very special thanks. You switch from child minder to computer expert to Karrimor partner with perfect ease and always with a sense of humour, which carries us a long way.

CONTENTS

INTRODUCTION

Discovering, using and enjoying new fresh ingredients has led to this book. I can't resist trying new food products; my insatiable curiosity turns the business of shopping into a great adventure. Often it's not all that obvious how to deal with something not encountered before. Are there hidden delights lurking behind a dull exterior? Will the cost really be worth it? Nevertheless, I always seem to be the one in the queue where the assistant is having to look up the individual bar codes as I've gone, yet again, for unfamiliar items.

I hope it will be clear from my choice of title that the emphasis in these vegetarian recipes is on *fresh*. Fresh, first and foremost in terms of the ingredients themselves, making the most of their bold flavours and natural textures. Fresh herbs, for example, can influence the taste of a dish, subtly or dramatically, in a way dried herbs seldom can. Fresh baby vegetables, tender and sweet, need just the briefest of cooking to be shown off at their best. Fresh cheeses, too, are now in abundance – light, smooth and rich all at the same time. How did I manage without them? Then there are fresh pastas, fresh exotic mushrooms, and so the list goes on.

I've also used the word fresh to mean *new*. Daily, intriguing and exotic products reach our shops from all over the world, bringing with them a wealth of flavours and fragrances but above all authenticity. This makes it more possible than ever to catch the spirit of far-off cuisines; the warmth of the Mediterranean shines through with sun-dried tomatoes and brilliant green pesto. You can capture a hint of the Orient with lemon grass, fresh ginger and furnace-like chillies.

It's true that many of the products I have used have been in some of the largest supermarkets for a while and in that sense are not all that new. What is different, compared with when I first started writing ten years ago, is the general availability of many unusual ingredients. When I wrote my first book, hazelnuts were hard to obtain. Now they are commonplace – not only plain or roasted, but in the form of sweet and delicious hazelnut oil too. A glance along

4

the shelves these days reveals a host of other oils and nuts as well, from pine kernels to fresh pistachios. Ease of access to all these items makes me feel free to use them without the worry that the minute I mention something like cold-pressed virgin olive oil, all my readers are having to book a trip to Tuscany.

Once home with my basket of goodies, I find the best of these ingredients are an inspiration. The tastes and textures are so good that often things need little nurturing and certainly no disguising. This makes for a light approach and quick cooking using old techniques such as grilling and roasting in new ways which keep the freshness of the ingredients.

This book has been great fun to write and I hope the end result for you is lots of new ideas, and plenty of colourful, fresh food.

How to Use This Book

As the ideas in this book have been inspired by ingredients, in most chapters I've grouped recipes together which use a group of foods. Information about individual ingredients and recipes follow each other, in most cases alphabetically. For example, in the chapter Fresh Herbs, I've given a detailed description of a particular herb, such as basil, and followed that with some recipes that make good use of it. But of course, use of an ingredient is not confined to one chapter. Fresh herbs, for example, crop up throughout the book in other recipes.

Each of the first eleven chapters includes a variety of savoury recipes. The range depends on the subject. In the chapters on spices for instance, there are recipes for soups, light meals and main courses. With pasta, I've concentrated more on sauces and main meals.

Following these ingredient-led chapters there are chapters for breads and special puddings. Following those, I've put together specific chapters on summer fare, barbecues, and Christmas and festive fare. Finally, at the back of the book you will find my suggestions for menus which take a seasonal theme.

Looking for a Recipe?

At the end of the book, I've given a complete list of recipes in the conventional order of soups, starters, salads, accompaniments and so on. If you want to make a particular type of recipe, you can find it there.

If you want to use a particular ingredient, either go straight to the appropriate chapter or look in the index.

Notes on Recipes

- All the recipes in this book have been tested.

- Follow one set of measurements only. Do not mix metric and imperial.

- Use size 3 eggs except where a large egg is needed. Then use size 1 or 2.

- Spoon measures are level unless otherwise stated.

- The type of oil to use in the recipe is generally indicated. For olive oil, use either virgin olive oil or a pure olive oil if you wish.

- The type of flour to use in the recipes is generally indicated but wholemeal flour and white flours are virtually interchangeable – the amount of liquid used and cooking times may vary slightly.

- Try to use fresh ingredients where I have indicated them. If you can only get a dried equivalent, the recipe will generally work, but the flavour may not be quite the same. Manufacturers are constantly coming up with new ways of preserving foods, such as freeze drying, and it is worth experimenting with these products.

- Servings are mostly for 4 people, but if you know you have a hungry family, increase quantities accordingly.

- Some ideas have been given on recipes that go well together. Many recipes that are so-called 'starters' work just as well as main courses but you will need to make extra quantities, or serve them with one or two other 'starters'.

FRESH HERBS

Fresh herbs, fragile and fleeting ingredients but what a difference they make. A hint of the Mediterranean with the warm pungency of oregano and thyme, the clean freshness of mint, an aromatic flavour of bay leaf spreading through a slowly simmering casserole. At one time, fresh herbs were used to disguise the awfulness of food. Now they are the ingredients that can enhance or enrich, dominate or almost disappear leaving a subtle undertone.

I don't think there are, or should be, any hard-and-fast rules when it comes to herbs. True, some herbs do have a strong affinity with a particular food. Try mushrooms cooked with marjoram for example or basil and oregano with tomatoes. In general, it is a matter of experimentation and personal taste, the two things which sum up the fun of cooking.

Buying Herbs

Do use fresh herbs. With few exceptions, their flavour is infinitely superior to anything dried. The cheapeast way to do this is to get plants and grow your own. No, this is not a gardening book! But I have to say herbs don't necessarily demand a garden. They will grow well in small spaces such as window-boxes, tubs and even on the kitchen window-sill. They need sunshine and protection from cold winds.

If you can't grow any, buy the growing pots of fresh herbs which are a welcome addition to some supermarket shelves. Look for mature plants that have a fair amount of growth. With a little care these can last well.

Specialist shops such as Indian, Greek or Italian grocers are good places to look for cut herbs. Large fresh bunches are often available. Failing that it is a matter of picking out the best of the plastic supermarket packs.

Storing Herbs

Cut herbs should be kept in the refrigerator or their stems chopped and put in water like a bunch of flowers. They should last a few days like this.

For long-term storage if you have your own herbs it is worth drying them. Spread out the leaves or sprigs on a rack and leave them in a dry, airy place. Once dried, take

7

the leaves off the stalks and pack into jars. Herbs that should still have a good flavour once dried are: bay leaves, marjoram, oregano, rosemary, thyme and sage.

Freezing herbs works quite well for some of the more fragile specimens. Again this applies if you have your own in abundant quantities. Freeze whole leaves or sprigs in polythene bags. Herbs that freeze fairly well are basil, chervil, parsley and tarragon. Infusing oil or vinegar with herbs is a wonderful way to keep their flavour. See pages 80–1.

Using Fresh Herbs

When to add herbs in cooking very much depends on the nature of the dish and choice of herb. Mostly you'll get a stronger flavour if herbs are added at the end of cooking or indeed sprinkled over a finished dish. This particularly applies to delicate flavours such as chervil or dill. For adding depth of flavour, herbs can also be added early on in the cooking of dishes such as sauces and casseroles. This works well with more pungent specimens such as marjoram, oregano and thyme. If you have to use dried herbs, always allow plenty of time for them to rejuvenate.

I can't really imagine cooking without herbs so they crop up throughout this book. I hope you'll make some discoveries as they hit your tastebuds. In this chapter I've dealt in detail with some of my favourites.

Basil

The best basil is grown in hot countries as it needs a lot of warmth to bring out its unique flavour. Its smell is wonderful, aromatic and slightly spicy, and that is just how it tastes. The oil in basil is volatile and lost in prolonged heating so it's best to add it towards the end of cooking.

Basil can be grown in cooler climates but remember that, even in the sunniest green-house, you won't be able to imitate the Mediterranean sun, so the herb may not be so powerful. Basil sold in a supermarket pot is often a good buy as the plants can be quite prolific.

The most familiar basil is Sweet Basil with its large green leaves. Other basils are becoming more popular, though at the moment they are more likely to be found in garden centres rather than in the shops. Look for Purple Basil which has just as good a flavour but a more dramatic colour.

Basil is a central ingredient in the classic Genoese sauce, pesto. I've used basil throughout this book, particularly in the oils and the pasta chapters.

Pesto

It would be impossible to write a chapter on herbs without mentioning pesto: this rich green sauce with its distinctive flavour of basil.

Ready-made pesto is widely available in supermarkets but I find the flavour of this is often disappointing as there seem to be too many bulking ingredients. A freshly made pesto from an Italian delicatessen or specialist food shop should be better. You can of course make your own very easily. Apart from basil, the main ingredients are usually garlic, pine kernels, olive oil and fresh Parmesan. Once you have the basic idea, it is worth experimenting with variations using parsley, cashew nuts, or pecorino cheese for example. Red pesto is made with sun-dried tomatoes. Home-made pesto should be kept in the refrigerator where it can be stored for up to two weeks.

I put a spoonful or two of pesto into many recipes such as sauces, salad dressings, dips and casseroles. It is lovely baked on bread for bruschetta, then topped with goat's cheese or ripe tomatoes, or used in sandwiches.

MAKES 150 ml (5 fl oz)

25 g (1 oz) pine kernels
50 g (2 oz) fresh basil leaves
2 cloves garlic, peeled
3–4 tablespoons olive oil

50 g (2 oz) fresh Parmesan
Salt and freshly ground black pepper

Blend the pine kernels, basil, garlic and oil together until smooth and creamy. Grate in the Parmesan and mix in well. Season to taste. Store in a clean screw-top jar.

For a smoother consistency, blend the pine kernels with the basil, garlic and grated Parmesan. Then add the oil gradually, blending thoroughly, before seasoning to taste.

Tender Vegetable Soup with Pesto

This quickly made soup relies on well-flavoured vegetables. I like to use baby carrots, fresh beans and small sweet courgettes. The last-minute addition of pesto adds a creamy taste and texture.

SERVES 4

2 tablespoons olive oil
1 onion, chopped
1 clove garlic, peeled and crushed
175 g (6 oz) baby carrots, chopped
175 g (6 oz) fine green beans, chopped
175 g (6 oz) courgettes, chopped

150 g (5 oz) button mushrooms
750–900 ml (1¼–1½ pints) vegetable stock
50 g (2 oz) small dried pasta shapes
3–4 tablespoons pesto
Salt and freshly ground black pepper

Heat the oil and gently cook the onion and garlic until translucent. Add the vegetables and cook slowly for 10–15 minutes, then pour over the stock and cook for a further 10–15 minutes or until the vegetables are quite tender. Add the pasta and cook until the pasta is just tender.

Just before serving stir in the pesto and season to taste. Serve hot.

Bay Leaf

My pride and joy is my Sweet Bay grown from a small sprig and now starting to earn the title tree. Bay leaves are one of the three herbs traditionally used in bouquet garni. They add a slightly spicy flavour to food. When cooked with rice, I think a bay leaf enhances the nutty flavour of the grain. A bay leaf should always be added early on in cooking as it takes time for the leaves to release their flavour. It is a herb which dries successfully.

Three Cheese Pizza

The thick tomato pulp on the base of this pizza is cooked with bay and thyme and has a warm pungent flavour.

Sun-dried tomatoes are halves of tomato dried in the sun, like dried fruit. Their flavour more than hints at what it must be like to have truly sun-ripened tomatoes rather than the flavourless greenhouse imports that we suffer today.

You can buy sun-dried tomatoes loose or preserved in oil which I prefer as they are softer. I also buy a sun-dried tomato paste which is pounded sun-dried tomatoes with oil. This is easy to incorporate into sauces and casseroles and makes an excellent flavouring.

SERVES 4

1 quantity Pizza Dough with
Olive Oil (page 193)

For the topping

3 tablespoons olive oil	1 teaspoon chopped fresh thyme
2 medium onions, finely chopped	2 tablespoons chopped fresh basil
2 cloves garlic, peeled and crushed	Salt and freshly ground black pepper
2 tablespoons sun-dried tomato paste	100 g (4 oz) mozzarella, sliced
1 × 400 g (14 oz) tin chopped tomatoes	50 g (2 oz) dolcelatte, cut in small pieces
1 bay leaf	25–50 g (1–2 oz) Parmesan, grated

First make the dough. Then heat the oil and gently fry the onion and garlic until very soft. Add the sun-dried tomato paste, tinned tomatoes, bay leaf and thyme and cook for 20–30 minutes over a gentle heat. The mixture should reduce to a thick pulp. Remove the bay leaf. Mix in the basil and season well. Roll the dough into a 25 cm (10 in) circle. Prick with a fork. Place on an oiled baking sheet. Spread the tomato topping over the pizza base. Arrange the slices of mozzarella over the top, dot with the dolcelatte pieces, then sprinkle over the Parmesan. Leave for at least 30 minutes so that the base is well risen while you pre-heat the oven to 200°C/400°F/gas 6.

Bake the pizza for 20–30 minutes or until the base is cooked and the cheese melted.

Chervil

Chervil is a pretty, delicate-looking herb with a refreshing, slightly aniseed flavour. It is one of the herbs used in the traditional French *fines herbes* mixture which consists of equal parts of chervil, chives, parsley and tarragon. The most familiar use of this mixture is probably in omelette *fines herbes*.

Chervil has enough flavour to stand on its own. Don't be afraid to use generous quantities. Its refreshing taste marries well with creamy ingredients.

Courgette and Chervil Galette with Lemon

Chervil looses much of its flavour if overcooked. In this filling made from courgettes and cream, it is added at the end and then heated through. Layer the filling with pancakes to produce a galette. It is easy to do and looks great.

Serves 4

For the pancakes

300 ml (10 fl oz) milk
1 egg
1 teaspoon oil

100 g (4 oz) plain flour
A pinch of salt
A little oil for frying

For the filling

2 tablespoons sunflower oil
100 g (4 oz) shallots, chopped
450 g (1 lb) courgettes, finely grated
Salt and freshly ground black pepper

2 eggs
150 ml (5 fl oz) single cream
1–2 tablespoons chopped fresh chervil
Zest of 1 lemon

Using a food processor or blender to make the pancakes, mix the milk, egg and oil together for 30 seconds. Then add the flour and salt and blend again until smooth. Leave the batter to stand for 20 minutes.

Using a small, preferably non-stick, frying-pan, heat a little oil and when the pan is smoking, add 2 tablespoons batter and fry the pancake for 2–3 minutes on each side. Leave to cool on a flat surface or plate. Make another 7 pancakes in the same way.

For the filling, heat the oil and fry the shallots until soft. Add the grated courgettes and cook until tender and most of the liquid has evaporated. Drain if necessary. Season to taste. Put the eggs, cream, chervil and lemon zest in a bowl and whisk together. Stir into the courgette mixture.

Grease and line an 18 cm (7 inch) deep spring-form tin. Pre-heat the oven to 190°C/375°F/gas 5.

Put 1 pancake in the bottom of the tin, cover with 2–3 tablespoons of courgette mixture, then put on another pancake. Continue to layer using the remaining mixture and pancakes, finishing with a pancake. Cover with foil, bake for 30 minutes. Serve hot.

Chives

Chives have to be fresh. Springy in texture with a mild oniony flavour, dried chives are a poor shadow of their former selves.

They can't really take any cooking either so reserve chives for uncooked dips, dressing and salads.

They will grow well. Use rich soil and give them full sun. You'll not only be rewarded with the herb but with pretty, purple-blue flowers.

Coriander

I love the strong heady scent of fresh coriander. It hits you the moment you begin chopping its leaves. Despite being such a powerful herb, it can be partnered with a multitude of savoury foods. Coriander originated in the Eastern Mediterranean, but its versatility has made it a jet-setter travelling the world to be part of such diverse cuisines as Indian, Mexican, and Thai.

There is no substitute for fresh coriander. Dried versions are available but they are as their name suggests, dry and dull. It is best to try to buy coriander from an ethnic shop. Here they are used to it being used in vast quantities and sell it in large bunches accordingly. The fresh growing pots of coriander in supermarkets are variable. A mature plant is a good buy, but often the plant is very young, the leaves are frail and frankly you don't get much. It is worth buying plants well in advance and leaving them to grow awhile before stripping them. Coriander is easy to grow from seed or, for the not so green-fingered, start with a plant from a garden centre. As a last resort, buy the pre-packaged coriander, but it is expensive.

I've used coriander extensively throughout this book, as a last-minute addition to curries and spiced dishes, in salads, in dips and sauces.

Tortilla with Coriander and Parsley

A tortilla is like a large flat omelette with a more solid texture than the classic recipe. As with all egg dishes, I find it is better with lots of flavourings or it is just bland. I've added lots of coriander and parsley to enliven the colour as well as perk up the flavour. A fresh creamy goat's cheese beaten into the eggs adds a subtle tang.

Don't be afraid of flipping the whole omelette over, it is easier than it sounds. Just be sure to start off with a plate or lid that is big enough.

SERVES 4

450 g (1 lb) potatoes, scrubbed
4 tablespoons olive oil
1 onion, finely chopped
1 clove garlic, peeled and crushed
6 large eggs (size 2)
150 g (5 oz) fresh goat's cheese
4 tablespoons chopped fresh parsley
4 tablespoons chopped fresh coriander
Salt and freshly ground black pepper
1 tablespoon oil

Par-boil the potatoes for 10 minutes, then drain well and slice. In a large frying-pan, heat the oil and fry the onion and garlic with the potato slices.

Beat the eggs and beat in the goat's cheese and herbs. Season very well. Pour this mixture over the potatoes and cook on a low heat for 20–30 minutes. Using a lid or plate larger than the frying-pan, tip the pan upside-down so that the tortilla drops on to the lid. Add a further tablespoon of oil to the pan and slide the tortilla back in to cook on the other side for 10 minutes. Serve in wedges either hot or at room temperature.

PREVIOUS PAGES
Left: *Roasted Baby Sweetcorn with Rosemary* (page 20)
Right: *Tortilla with Coriander and Parsley* (page 16)

Dill

Dill is a feathery, fragrant herb with an almost sweet aromatic flavour. It is from the same family as fennel as are some of the other aniseed-flavoured herbs such as chervil, caraway and anise. Fresh dill works best if added at the last minute as it does lose its flavour if cooked for too long. Dill also adds a pleasant flavour to green salads, is good with cucumber and goes well with cream, cheese and similar dairy products.

Crisp Buttered Vegetables with Dill and Parsley

Dill adds a refreshing taste to these soft buttery vegetables. It is added at the end to keep its flavour.

SERVES 4

225–275 g (8–10 oz) fennel
225 g (8oz) carrots
100 g (4 oz) fine beans
50 g (2 oz) butter
2 tablespoons chopped fresh dill

2 tablespoons chopped fresh parsley
Salt and freshly ground black pepper

Chop the fennel finely. Peel the carrots and chop in ovals. Trim the beans and chop into thirds.

Melt the butter and sweat the vegetables for 10 minutes or until they are just beginning to soften. Stir in the herbs and season well. Serve immediately.

Marjoram and Oregano

These two herbs do need mentioning in the same breath as they are from the same family and have similar aromatic peppery qualities. Oregano is slightly more pungent. Both herbs are native to the Mediterranean. Their warmth and robust character is a perfect foil for all the food typical of that region: tomatoes, aubergines, capers and olives. Both marjoram and oregano can stand a certain amount of cooking. In those instances, the dried varieties of the herbs work tolerably well.

Try blending marjoram and oregano with other strong herbs such as bay, rosemary and thyme.

Courgette and Green Olive Soup

Olives are not commonly used in soups but I find their acidity brings out the flavour of other ingredients. In addition their natural oil has a velvet texture. Green olives in particular give soup a wonderful rich colour.

SERVES 4

2 tablespoons olive oil
1 onion, chopped
1 clove garlic, peeled and crushed
750 g (1½ lb) courgettes, chopped
½ teaspoon chopped fresh thyme
½ teaspoon chopped fresh
    oregano

1 bay leaf
50 g (2 oz) pitted green olives
750 ml (1¼ pint) vegetable stock
2–3 tablespoons lemon juice
Salt and freshly ground black
    pepper

Heat the oil and gently cook the onion and garlic until soft. Add the courgettes and sweat for 10 minutes. Then add the herbs, olives and stock. Bring to the boil and simmer for 25–30 minutes or until the courgettes are really soft. Leave to cool then blend or sieve until smooth. Add the lemon juice and season well. Re-heat before serving.

Mint

Mint is a herb that shouldn't be limited to a sauce! It has a splendid fresh, lively taste, and is easy to grow. Too easy perhaps. It needs confining to a pot or tub or you will find mint taking over the garden. Its clean flavour works well with starchy foods such as bulgar wheat in the classic salad dish *Tabbouleh* (page 77). I also like mint with highly spiced dishes where it has a cooling effect. Add it in the final few moments of cooking to get the best results. A little mint adds another dimension to a plain green leafy salad.

Pink Fir Apple Potatoes
with Mint Salsa

In this recipe, I have used mint in plentiful quantities mixed with olive oil and tossed into freshly cooked potatoes. The warmth of the potatoes really brings out the flavour of the herbs.

If you can get Pink Fir Apple potatoes, snap them up. They have slightly yellow flesh, a wonderful waxy texture, and rounded nutty flavour. Ratte (rarely seen) is another new potato worth looking for.

450–750 g (1–1½ lb) Pink Fir
    Apple potatoes or new
    potatoes
5 tablespoons finely chopped
    fresh mint

3 tablespoons finely chopped
    fresh parsley
6 tablespoons olive oil
½ teaspoon salt
Freshly ground black pepper

Scrub the potatoes and boil or steam them until just tender.

Meanwhile prepare the salsa. Mix the mint and parsley with the olive oil and salt, then add black pepper to taste. Immediately the potatoes are cooked, drain them if necessary and toss in the salsa. Serve hot.

Parsley

At last, I thought partriotically, a British herb! But no, parsley, though certainly naturalized in Britain, first grew in south-eastern Europe. The flat-leafed variety still grown on the Continent closely resembles coriander. In fact I think it helps to think of parsley as a foreigner. It might then be treated more adventurously instead of being left to lead a life of culinary garnishing.

The colour of fresh parsley is wonderful. It is relatively cheap too so should be used in abundance. It combines well with other herbs such as coriander and mint. Add parsley to casseroles early on, as with bouquet garni, or add at the end to steamed vegetables, use sprigs in salads, or chop and blend into creamy dips. Really there are few foods parsley will clash with and so many it will improve.

Luckily fresh parsley is readily available. I'm even able to get an organically grown variety. Dried parsley is a waste of time.

Rosemary

Rosemary is native to the eastern Mediterranean, although it grows extremely well in other climates too. It does go well with foods from the Mediterranean but seems to have been overshadowed by oregano, marjoram and thyme. I think it is worth using rosemary instead to ring the changes. Be sure to chop rosemary well or the needles can be spiky. Dried rosemary has a reasonable flavour.

Roasted Baby Sweetcorn with Rosemary

Roasted rosemary has a wonderful flavour. It goes well with sweetcorn
in this very simple side dish. It is also good with roasted new potatoes.
Serve this dish hot as a side vegetable or starter, or leave to cool
and use in a salad.

SERVES 4

225 g (8 oz) baby sweetcorn
1 tablespoon sunflower oil
1 tablespoon chopped fresh
*   rosemary*
Salt and freshly ground black
*   pepper*

Pre-heat the oven to 200°C/400°F/gas 6.

Trim the sweetcorn and toss in a small bowl with the oil, rosemary and seasoning until
well coated.

Place the sweetcorn on a baking sheet covered with baking parchment and roast for
10–12 minutes. Serve hot or cold.

Sage

Sage, fresh or dried, is a powerful herb which can dominate a dish but equally it can
lend a distinctive taste to bland mixtures. Its pungency cuts through fatty flavours and
for this reason I think it ideal in foods such as rissoles which are fried. Sage doesn't lose
its flavour after long cooking and so it is a herb that is also useful in casserole-style
dishes. Whole fresh sage leaves taste good roasted.

Leek and Pecan Fritters with Fresh Sage

The strong taste of sage works very well with these easy fritters. Celery
seeds, which are also in the recipe, have a similar but more intense
flavour than celery itself.

SERVES 4

1 tablespoon olive oil
225 g (8oz) leeks, cleaned and
shredded
1 shallot, diced
½ teaspoon celery seeds
25 g (1 oz) plain wholemeal flour
25 g (1 oz) pecan nuts

1 teaspoon chopped fresh sage
Salt and freshly ground black
pepper
2 eggs, separated
3–4 tablespoons sunflower oil
for frying

Pre-heat the oven to 200°C/400°F/gas 6.

Heat the olive oil and sauté the leeks and shallot until the leeks have just wilted but are still bright green. Stir in the celery seeds and flour and cook for 2 minutes.

Meanwhile, toast the pecan nuts in the oven for 3–5 minutes then chop them finely.

Take the leeks and shallot off the heat and stir the pecan nuts into the mixture. Add the sage and seasoning, then beat in the egg yolks. Whisk the egg whites until stiff, but not dry, then fold into the leek mixture.

Heat the sunflower oil and fry the fritter mixture using 1 heaped tablespoon for each fritter. Cook for 4–5 minutes on each side. Serve hot.

Tarragon

French tarragon is a bushy plant with slender leaves. It has a delicate flavour which is only apparent when the herb is fresh. Whilst it is not a herb I have permanently on my shopping list, I do like using tarragon-flavoured oils and vinegars. These add a special flavour to dressings, dips and the like.

Thyme

This pungent herb is a favourite of mine. I like its versatility. Sometimes I combine it with its Mediterranean friends, marjoram and oregano. But it's equally at home with the flavours of parsley, sage and bay leaves. Its flavour is concentrated and when dried it can be musty and ruin a dish. It is best to use thyme fresh and then be more liberal with it.

OVERLEAF
Left: Crisp Buttered Vegetables with Dill and Parsley (page 17)
Right: Salsa Verde with Grilled Vegetables (page 24)

Salsa Verde

Salsa verde is an olive oil-based dressing packed with fresh herbs. It is best made in the summer when herbs such as basil are plentiful. You can only use fresh herbs and certainly shouldn't skimp. Many herbs are suitable for this dish, particularly parsley, basil, oregano, thyme, marjoram, chives, dill and tarragon.

Use this sauce over a single vegetable such as globe artichokes, new potatoes or fine beans. Salsa verde is also good with barbecued vegetables. Any left-over salsa will keep in the refrigerator. It may lose its bright colour and separate slightly. Use within two or three days.

MAKES 200 ml (7 fl oz)

50 g (2 oz) mixed fresh herbs
150 ml (5 fl oz) olive oil
Juice of 1–2 lemons

1 clove garlic, peeled and crushed
Salt and freshly ground black pepper

Chop the fresh herbs very finely. Mix together the olive oil, lemon juice and garlic, then stir in the herbs and season well.

Salsa Verde with Grilled Vegetables

I like a colourful mixture of grilled vegetables for a light main course served with bread.

SERVES 4

1 quantity Salsa Verde

For the vegetables

A little olive oil
Salt and freshly ground black pepper
12 baby sweetcorn, trimmed

4 artichoke hearts in oil, halved
4 small courgettes, cut lengthways
2 Italian beef tomatoes, sliced

Season the olive oil and toss the prepared vegetables in it. Put them under a moderate grill and cook until tender: the vegetables that need the most cooking should be cooked first. Start with the sweetcorn, then add the artichokes, courgettes and tomato slices.

Serve the hot vegetables with Salsa Verde spooned over the top.

FUNGI

Mushrooms – almost as elusive as fresh herbs in some respect and yet they can be the heartiest and 'meatiest' part of a vegetarian diet. There are two distinct fungi groups I'll deal with: wild mushrooms, most readily available dried; and fresh cultivated mushrooms. Here are some preliminary guidelines on mushrooms starting with wild and followed by fresh.

Wild Mushrooms

Whilst fresh wild mushrooms are beginning to appear in the large supermarkets, in this book I have only concentrated on the dried varieties: ceps, chanterelles (or girolles), morels, and *trompettes de mort*. Obviously all of them have been fresh somewhere and at some time. Some, like the chanterelle, can be found in this country and mushroom foraging can be great fun. But it can also be hazardous unless you can positively identify the fungus as being edible. Although you have to pay for them, the advantage of buying wild mushrooms dried is that they are definitely safe to eat and available all year round, even if only by mail order!

Buying Dried Mushrooms

Dried wild mushrooms at first glance seem wildly expensive. It is worth shopping around, probably avoiding supermarkets and heading straight for delicatessens or Italian shops. Here the mushrooms may be sold loose and can be cheaper. Remember, too, that you do only need very small quantities. As they are dried, these mushrooms will keep almost indefinitely in a dry place.

How to Prepare Dried Mushrooms

Dried mushrooms must always be soaked in some sort of liquid – boiling water, wine, lemon juice or what you will. This process is partly necessary to clean the mushrooms. As they open out during soaking, earthy particles can float out or certainly be removed more easily. It does sound a labour of love to start any recipe, 'first clean your mushroom gills', but any left-over grit will ruin the dish. Ceps take about 20 minutes to soak properly, the others around 15 minutes. Allow longer if you are using a cold liquid. Don't throw away the soaking liquid. It should already have that elusive mushroom flavour. Strain it well, preferably through coffee filters, and then add it to the dish.

To bring out the best flavour of the dried mushrooms once soaked, chop them, sauté in a little oil or butter, with a hint of garlic, then simmer them in some soaking liquid until tender.

Fresh Mushrooms

This group is increasingly more exotic and, as I've said, I've recently seen several types of wild mushroom sold fresh in the larger supermarkets. As the availability of these is still limited, I've concentrated here on the following: button, open cup, semi-open cup, chestnut, oyster, field and shitake mushrooms.

Buying and Storing Fresh Mushrooms

Fresh mushrooms should be *fresh*. To get the best it is a matter of picking and choosing and, to a certain extent, smelling. Mushrooms past their best do have a sour odour. They should look firm and any trace of sliminess is a bad sign. Shitake and oyster mushrooms are harder to judge before buying as they are generally pre-packed. It's best to be guided by the sell-by date and a thorough inspection of the packet.

Many shops now offer paper bags for storing mushrooms. These do work and will keep mushrooms fresher. Even so, store them in the fridge. If you buy pre-packed ones, help yourself to a bag anyway. Remove any polythene as soon as you can.

Cooking Fresh Mushrooms

The golden rule is wipe not wash. Do this with a cloth or soft brush. If you have to rinse, make it more of a swirl than a soak. Trim the ends if necessary with a knife.

Mushrooms do exude liquid as they cook. For soups and sauces, this doesn't matter as the flavour of the liquor will add to the overall taste of the dish. If you are using mushrooms for a filling and need a drier finish, reduce the liquid on a high heat, or pour off liquid as the mushrooms cook, adding more oil to the pan if necessary.

Ceps

These are also sold as 'porcini', which incidentally are not little pieces of pig! Beige in colour, these chunky mushrooms have a dense woody flavour. They are imported from Italy and France and are the most readily available dried mushroom. They have a spongy texture when reconstituted. They are best used finely sliced.

Ceps and Red Wine Soufflé

Ceps and a red wine reduction give this soufflé a strong flavour and good rich colour. For a starter serve it in individual ramekins and reduce the cooking time. For a main course, serve with a cream sauce, lightly steamed green vegetables such as broccoli florets, and new potatoes.

SERVES 4

15 g (½ oz) dried ceps
300 ml (10 fl oz) red wine
20 g (¾ oz) butter
20 g (¾ oz) plain flour
1 shallot, chopped

25 g (1 oz) butter
¼ teaspoon French mustard
3 eggs, separated
Salt and freshly ground black pepper

Soak the ceps in the red wine for 30 minutes. Drain well and rinse, then chop and set aside. Strain the wine. Boil the wine until it has reduced to 150 ml (5 fl oz).

Melt the butter and stir in the flour to make a roux, pour over the red wine and bring to the boil stirring frequently to make a thick sauce. Leave to cool.

Brown the shallot in the remaining butter, then add the chopped ceps and cook for a few minutes or until tender. Add these and the mustard to the wine sauce plus 3 egg yolks. Season very well.

Pre-heat the oven to 200°C/400°F/gas 6.

Whisk the egg whites until stiff but not dry, then fold into the wine sauce.

Pour into a greased 600 ml (1 pint) soufflé dish and bake for 25–30 minutes or until well risen and just firm in the centre. Serve immediately.

Chanterelles

These are dainty mushrooms – also known as girolles – which range in colour from pale yellow through gold to almost russet. They have a more delicate flavour than ceps.

Morels

The star of the mushroom world and priced accordingly. Whole dried morels once reconstituted look marvellous but dried pieces of morel, whilst not nearly so attractive, are cheaper. These will still impart an intense bouquet. Morels have a honeycombed cap that can be quite gritty so do clean them very carefully. Even after soaking, it's worth rinsing them under the tap.

Trompettes de mort

The dramatic name matches their appearance much more so than the placid 'horns of plenty' which is the English translation. These jet black slender trumpets have a good earthy flavour and yield a splendid richly-coloured stock. Incidentally they don't lose their colour as they cook. Their blackness looks good against a contrasting background.

Wild Mushroom Ragout

This recipe uses both fresh and dried mushrooms. Use as wide a range as you can lay your hands on. I hope the end result will show you some of the flavoursome possibilities of combining fresh and dried mushrooms. The dried ones impart an intense bouquet whilst the fresh mushrooms add texture and colour. Serve this with a simple risotto or plain rice or as a filling for pancakes.

SERVES 4

25 g (1 oz) mixed dried wild
   mushrooms
300 ml (10 fl oz) stock
2 tablespoons olive oil
1 teaspoon coriander seeds,
   lightly crushed
1 onion, finely chopped

2 cloves garlic, peeled and crushed
450 g (1 lb) mixed fresh
   mushrooms (such as chestnut
   and open-cup), chopped
3–4 sprigs of rosemary
Salt and freshly ground black
   pepper

Soak the dried mushrooms in the stock for about 30 minutes. Remove and rinse then chop finely and set aside. Strain the stock through a coffee filter to remove any sediment.

Heat the oil and gently toast the coriander seeds to release the aromas. Add the onion and garlic and cook until translucent. Then add the chopped fresh mushrooms and cook until soft. Next add the chopped dried mushrooms, about half the strained stock and the sprigs of rosemary. Bring to the boil and simmer for 30 minutes, uncovered, until most of the liquid has evaporated and the mushrooms are very tender. Season well and serve hot.

Wild Mushroom Stock

Dried mushrooms are marvellous for making a simple yet rich stock with complex flavours. This is one instance where I do not bother to soak the mushrooms first as all the ingredients have to be gently simmered to draw out the flavours. As with traditional stock, only the liquid is used. The stock must be thoroughly strained. The vegetables are discarded.

MAKES 800 ml (1½ pints)

1 tablespoon oil
1 onion, chopped
2 sticks celery, chopped
1 bay leaf

25 g (1 oz) mixed dried wild mushrooms
A sprig of fresh thyme

Heat the oil and fry the onion until lightly coloured. Add the remaining ingredients with 1.2 litres (2 pints) water and bring to the boil. Simmer, uncovered, for an hour until the mixture has reduced by about one quarter. Strain through a fine sieve or coffee filter.

OVERLEAF
Left: *Grilled Goat's Cheese with Oyster Mushrooms and Radicchio* (page 37)
Right: *Chestnut Mushroom Gourgère with Pecorino* (page 34)

Many Mushroom Sauce

It is worth taking the trouble to make *Wild Mushroom Stock* (page 29) for this special sauce. Use strong-flavoured fresh mushrooms for the body of the sauce, I suggest field, chestnut or shitake.

This sauce can certainly be used with Christmas recipes as well as with stuffed vegetables and pancakes.

SERVES 4

50 g (2 oz) butter
25 g (1 oz) plain flour
600 ml (1 pint) Wild Mushroom
*   Stock (see page 29)*
1 shallot, chopped
1 clove garlic, peeled and
*   crushed*
50 g (2 oz) fresh mushrooms,
*   finely chopped*

½ teaspoon fresh thyme,
*   chopped*
1 bay leaf
1 sprig of parsley
2 tablespoons red wine
Salt and freshly ground black
*   pepper*

Melt 25 g (1 oz) butter and sprinkle over the flour, stir and cook the roux and then add the mushroom stock. Bring to the boil and then simmer for 5 minutes.

In a separate pan, melt the remaining butter and gently cook the shallot and garlic until soft. Add the fresh mushrooms and cook for 5–6 minutes. Then add the herbs and wine and cook the mixture for 10 minutes. Scrape into the main pan of sauce and cook for 5 minutes. Season to taste.

Button Mushrooms

Button mushrooms, open-cap, semi open-cap and closed cap, are the commonest culti-vated mushrooms. Once thought of as a luxury, they seem to have held their price in relation to many other ingredients.

They are good for absorbing as well as giving flavour. Their texture, raw and cooked, is splendid. I think, unless you want a particular size of mushroom, they are virtually interchangeable. However, when I want the palest of results, as in the follow-ing pâté, I choose the button mushroom which is delicately coloured throughout.

Mushroom Parfait with Mascarpone and White Wine

This rich pâté has a melt-in-the-mouth texture. Serve it in thin slices with crisp biscuits or thin toast.

SERVES 6–8

50 g (2 oz) butter
2 cloves garlic, peeled and crushed
2 shallots, chopped
½ teaspoon caraway seeds
350 g (12 oz) button mushrooms

150 ml (5 fl oz) white wine
100 g (4 oz) mascarpone cheese
Salt and freshly ground black pepper
Sprigs of watercress to garnish

Melt 25 g (1 oz) butter and cook the garlic and shallots for about 10 minutes or until thoroughly soft. Add the caraway seeds and mushrooms and continue cooking for 5 minutes, then pour over the wine. Continue cooking over a high heat, stirring constantly, until the mushrooms have softened and all the liquid has evaporated. Leave until completely cold.

Purée the mushroom mixture with the remaining butter and mascarpone. Season to taste. Put in a small cling film lined dish (margarine tub size) and leave to chill.

Turn out on to a small dish and garnish with watercress.

Chestnut Mushrooms

I first bought chestnut mushrooms because they were one of the few organically grown products that were cheaper than their non-organic equivalent. Now everyone has cottoned on to their delicious flavour and is used to the fact that mushrooms needn't necessarily be white, I've noticed their price has gone up.

Chestnut mushrooms are the colour of their name, they have a good dense texture and darken on cooking. Small ones, kept whole, can look dramatic in casseroles and sauces.

Chestnut Mushroom Gougère with Pecorino

Choose small chestnut mushrooms for this recipe, preferably those with a closed cup. Then leave the mushrooms whole in this filling as they will look both dramatic and attractive.

I like the dry flavour of pecorino cheese in the choux pastry which makes the gougère. A good final touch is to grate a little over the finished dish.

SERVES 4

For the gougère pastry

150 ml (5 fl oz) water
50 g (2 oz) butter
50 g (2 oz) plain flour

2 eggs
50 g (2 oz) fresh pecorino, grated
¼ teaspoon prepared mustard

For the filling

2 tablespoons oil
1 onion, chopped
2 sticks celery, diced
1 red pepper, de-seeded and chopped

350 g (12 oz) small whole chestnut mushrooms
4–6 tablespoons passata (see page 124)
Salt and freshly ground black pepper

Extra grated pecorino to serve

For the gougère pastry, put the water and the butter in a saucepan and bring to the boil. When boiling and the butter is melted, remove the pan from the heat and shoot in all the flour. Beat until very glossy. Beat in the eggs one at a time. Next add the cheese and mustard and beat again.

Pre-heat the oven to 200°C/400°F/gas 6.

Put the mixture in spoonfuls around a lightly-greased flan dish. Bake for 20 minutes, then reduce the oven temperature to 190°C/375°F/gas 5 and bake for a further 5–10 minutes. It is best if the pastry is quite crisp or it can collapse.

Meanwhile make the filling. Heat the oil and cook the onion and celery until fairly soft but not coloured. Add the red pepper and whole mushrooms and fry more quickly until the mushrooms soften. Turn the heat down and continue to cook until the mushrooms are quite soft, then pour over the passata. Stir and season well. Keep warm.

When the gougère is cooked, pile the filling into the middle and serve sprinkled with extra pecorino.

Field Mushrooms

Sometimes the size of a saucer, these mushrooms have a mild flavour and juicy melting flesh. They can be chopped for sauces and the like but their shape makes them ideal for stuffing. Topping would be a more accurate description, as it is the stalk which is removed and any filling is piled on top.

Stuffed Field Mushrooms with Red Pesto

This is a good quick first course or part of a light main meal. Choose firm flat field mushrooms for this recipe. The full-flavoured filling is very quick to make in a food processor. Red pesto is available in larger supermarkets or use green instead (see page 9).

SERVES 4

4 field mushrooms
1 red pepper
2 tablespoons olive oil
1 onion, finely chopped
2 cloves garlic, peeled and crushed
8 sun-dried tomatoes (in oil)

100 g (4 oz) black olives, pitted
2 teaspoons red pesto
4 tablespoons chopped fresh basil
Salt and freshly ground black pepper
3–4 teaspoons Parmesan

Pre-heat the oven to 190°C/375°F/gas 5.

Wipe the field mushrooms and remove the stalks. Chop the stalks finely and set aside.

Wipe the red pepper and brush with a little oil. Bake for 40 minutes or until the skin is well-charred. Leave to cool then peel off the skin and remove the seeds.

To make the filling, heat the remaining oil and fry the onion and garlic until soft, add the chopped mushroom stalks and cook for 2–3 minutes. Put the remaining ingredients including the red pepper into a food processor. Add the cooked onion mix and process until finely chopped. Season to taste. Pile the filling into the mushrooms. Place on a shallow tray and sprinkle a little grated Parmesan over each mushroom. Bake for 15 minutes. Serve hot.

Oyster Mushrooms

The oyster mushroom is the belle of the ball. It has a pretty fluted shape, pale grey gills or sometimes pastel yellow. The two colours taste the same, both quite delicate but with a succulent flesh. They exude a good deal of liquid so be prepared for shrinkage.

Oyster Mushrooms in Parmesan Crêpes

Oyster mushrooms and mascarpone cheese make a rich melting filling. If you can find tiny oyster mushrooms, leave them whole as they look so pretty. If there is too much liquid as you cook the mushrooms pour some away or the filling will be diluted.

Serves 4

For the pancakes

300 ml (10 fl oz) milk
1 egg
1 teaspoon oil
4 tablespoons grated Parmesan

125 g (4 oz) plain white
  flour
A pinch of salt
Oil for frying

For the filling

2 tablespoons olive oil
50 g (2 oz) shallots, chopped
1 clove garlic, peeled and crushed
225 g (8 oz) oyster mushrooms,
  thickly sliced
100 g (4 oz) mascarpone cheese

1 tablespoon chopped fresh basil
2 tablespoons chopped fresh
  parsley
Salt and freshly ground black
  pepper
Extra grated Parmesan to serve

To make the pancakes, blend the milk, egg and oil in a food processor, then add the Parmesan, flour and salt. Blend again and allow the mixture to stand for 20 minutes or so before making the pancakes.

Using a small, preferably non-stick, frying-pan, heat a little oil and when the pan is smoking, add 2 tablespoons batter. Spread round the pan and then cook for 2–3 minutes on each side. Keep warm under some foil in a low oven. The batter should make 8–10 pancakes.

For the filling, heat the oil and gently cook the shallots and garlic until soft but not coloured. Add the oyster mushrooms and cook gently until soft. This takes about 10 minutes. Drain off excess liquid (save it for sauces). Quickly stir in the mascarpone cheese and herbs. Season to taste. Stuff each pancake with a little filling and roll up. Dust with extra Parmesan and serve immediately.

Grilled Goat's Cheese
with Oyster Mushrooms and Radicchio

The best goat's cheeses to use for this dish are called crottins. You may find several varieties on sale. Crottin browns wonderfully and melts well. Otherwise choose a cheese which is firm enough to slice. For more information on goat's cheese see pages 100, 107. Instead of plain olive oil for frying you could use a mixture of olive oil and chilli oil.

This is a light, colourful dish with plenty of flavour. Served with *Deep-fried Polenta* (page 136) it makes a more substantial meal.

SERVES 4

2 tablespoons olive oil
200 g (7 oz) oyster mushrooms
Salt and freshly ground black
*   pepper*
8–12 radicchio leaves

1 tablespoon Chilli Oil
*   (see page 80) for brushing*
*   leaves*
2 crottins, halved or 100 g (4 oz)
*   goat's cheese, sliced*

Heat the oil and fry the mushrooms with seasoning over a high heat until brown.

Brush the radicchio leaves with chilli oil and arrange on individual gratin dishes. Arrange the fried oyster mushrooms on the leaves and top with the goat's cheese. Finish with some extra black pepper. Flash under a hot grill and cook until the cheese is just melting. Serve immediately.

OVERLEAF
Stuffed Field Mushrooms
with Red Pesto (page 35)

Shitake Mushrooms

These oriental mushrooms are now cultivated in France and Holland giving us, as it were, local access to these hearty specimens. They are not regular or pretty to look at but shitake have a robust flavour and substantial texture. They are fine for sauces and casseroles but also work well in stir-fry dishes.

Stir-fry Shitake Mushrooms with Sharp Thai Sauce

Sharp citrus flavours spiked with chilli make a lively combination in this stir-fry. Small mushrooms can be left whole otherwise slice them thickly so as to keep a sense of their texture. Serve this light dish with rice or noodles.

SERVES 4

For the sauce

3–4 tablespoons lime juice
Zest of 1 lime
1–2 tablespoons shoyu
1 stem lemon grass, finely diced

3 tablespoons finely chopped
   fresh coriander
3–4 tablespoons water

For the stir-fry

2 tablespoons sunflower oil
2 cloves garlic, peeled and
   chopped
1 hot red chilli, de-seeded and
   diced
225 g (8 oz) shitake mushrooms,
   sliced

225 g (8 oz) baby sweetcorn,
   cut into large chunks
8 spring onions, finely
   chopped
Salt and freshly ground black
   pepper

Mix together all the ingredients for the sauce.

Heat the oil for the stir-fry and quickly fry the garlic and chilli. Add the vegetables and, keeping the heat high, stir and fry to prevent them burning. Do this until the mushrooms begin to soften, then pour over the sauce. Cover with a lid and leave to steam for 2–3 minutes. Season if necessary. Serve immediately.

BABY VEGETABLES

Baby vegetables are fun: egg-sized aubergines, cauliflowers not much bigger than a golf ball, finger-like carrots and tiny fluted squashes which are certainly the catch of the season. I think baby vegetables deserve their own chapter as their size does inspire a different way of cooking. Don't be fooled that because they are young, they will necessarily be tender and sweet. Tiny carrots and parsnips picked from your own garden may taste sweeter but baby aubergines, courgettes and leeks taste very like their senior counterparts. Any vegetable can be baby-sized, after all we've all got to start somewhere. Some work very well, such as cauliflower and patty pans. Baby fennel isn't so good. It's too large to eat at one go, and not small enough to be dainty. I thought baby peppers looked fun but only ever saw them once in the supermarket. Maybe they will return. As it is the size that is all-important, I would also include cherry tomatoes and button mushrooms amongst baby vegetables as they are both excellent used whole.

All the recipes in this chapter can, of course, also be made with larger vegetables. Just chop them accordingly.

OVERLEAF
Baby Aubergines in Spiced Tomato and Apricot Sauce (page 44)

41

Aubergines

Miniature ovals of aubergine make a wonderful focus for a dish. They taste very like a fully grown aubergine, although sometimes their colour is a less intense purple.

Left whole, they do take quite a time to cook. I find roasting them first helps to soften them, but they still retain their shape. Roasted until completely soft, baby aubergines are good served cold in salads. Barbecued baby aubergines are fun to try but it is best to give them a little pre-cooking first.

Baby Aubergines in Spiced Tomato and Apricot Sauce

This fruity sauce is backed up with a lively mixture of spices. The aubergines are softened first before being poached but they still have time to absorb the flavours in the sauce.

I serve these with a plain basmati rice with Greek yoghurt in a separate bowl.

SERVES 4

*8–12 baby aubergines
(depending on the size)*

For the sauce

*50 g (2 oz) dried apricots,
    snipped into slivers
300 ml (10 fl oz) boiling water
2 tablespoons Chilli Oil (see
    page 80)
1 teaspoon cumin seeds
1 onion, finely chopped
1 clove garlic, peeled and
    crushed*

*¼ teaspoon cayenne pepper or to
    taste
1 × 2.5 cm (1 inch) piece root
    ginger, peeled and grated
450 ml (15 fl oz) passata (see
    page 124)
2 tablespoons lemon juice
Salt and freshly ground black
    pepper*

Pre-heat the oven to 200°C/400°F/gas 6 and roast the aubergines for 15 minutes or until just soft.

For the sauce, put the apricots into a small saucepan and pour the boiling water over them. Cover and simmer for 10–15 minutes until fairly soft.

In a separate pan heat the oil and fry the cumin seeds for 1–2 minutes, then add the onion and garlic and cook until soft. Add the cayenne pepper, ginger, passata and lemon juice. Drain the apricots and add to the pan with 150 ml (5 fl oz) of their cooking liquid. Put in the whole aubergines and bring the mixture to the boil. Simmer for 30 minutes, season to taste, then serve hot.

Cauliflower

Baby cauliflowers are a delight, small but perfectly formed. Having been brought up to eat stalk and leaf of cauliflower senior, I always feel awful if I throw these bits away, yet if I don't I'm left struggling to make the florets look attractive. Serving one mini cauliflower, although pricey, solves these problems and saves waste. It is obviously pointless chopping up baby cauliflower for salads or casseroles. Make a feature of it by serving it as an 'in-between' before the main course.

Miniature Cauliflower with Saffron Sauce

Infusing saffron in wine for a few minutes brings out both its colour and flavour. This delicate golden sauce looks lovely with baby cauliflowers. This dish could make an unusual first course or serve it as a side dish.

SERVES 4

For the sauce

50 g (2 oz) butter
100 g (4 oz) shallots, chopped
2 tablespoons white wine
A large pinch of saffron
2 teaspoons chopped fresh thyme

5 g (½ oz) plain white flour
200 ml (7 fl oz) vegetable stock
Salt and freshly ground black pepper

4 miniature cauliflowers

Melt the butter and gently cook the shallots until very soft.

Add the white wine, saffron and thyme, cover the pan and cook for 5 minutes. Add the flour and stir in, then add the vegetable stock. Bring the sauce to the boil, stirring, and then simmer for 5 minutes. Season to taste. Steam or microwave the cauliflower for 5–6 minutes or until tender. Pour the sauce over the top and serve immediately.

Cherry Tomatoes

These aren't really baby vegetables but I've sneaked them in here. Whenever I'm writing about cherry tomatoes I tend to type the word cheery, but I think it is an apt mistake. They add a good splash of colour and, if you're lucky, a sweet mouthful of flavour.

I have experimented cooking with them. In some dishes, such as the poached recipe below, they work well. Even though the colour diminishes and they become a little misshapen, they still add that fresh sweet sharpness characteristic of tomatoes.

Courgettes

Baby courgettes should be firm and dark green with a more intense flavour than large courgettes. Certainly if ever I'm cooking courgettes (except if I'm stuffing them) I tend to look for the smaller ones as they taste better. Younger specimens need very little cooking.

Baby Vegetables
Poached in Fresh Herb Marinade

Use good-quality oil and fresh herbs for making this easy marinade. I have suggested poaching cherry tomatoes, baby courgettes and button mushrooms but other vegetables such as patty pans and baby sweetcorn work well. Instead of the courgettes you could also use chopped green beans. Prepare this recipe well in advance of eating, as the flavours need time to develop. Serve this as part of a salad meal, perhaps on a picnic. Provide lots of bread to mop up the juices.

SERVES 4

For the marinade

150 ml (5 fl oz) olive oil
150 ml (5 fl oz) white wine
1 bay leaf
3 teaspoons chopped fresh oregano
4 teaspoons chopped fresh thyme

4 cloves garlic, peeled and thinly sliced
½–1 teaspoon salt or to taste
2 teaspoons lightly crushed coriander seeds

275 g (10 oz) cherry tomatoes
225 g (8 oz) baby courgettes
225 g (8 oz) button mushrooms
Salt and freshly ground black
pepper

Put all the ingredients for the marinade in a wide shallow pan. Add the vegetables. There should be enough room in the pan to have them in one layer.

Bring the mixture to the boil and simmer for 5 minutes, turning the vegetables over once or twice. Leave to cool in the marinade. Season to taste.

Baby Sweetcorn

Baby or dwarf sweetcorn has suffered rather from being the first baby vegetable to reach stardom. Don't neglect it. It brightens up stews and stir-fry dishes as well as being delicious roasted (see page 20).

Baby Vegetables in Filo Shells with Crème Fraîche

Filo pastry is a wonderfully versatile ingredient. I buy it rather than make it as it is virtually impossible to roll out such paper-fine sheets. You will find filo in the freezer section of the supermarket and in some Greek or Cypriot shops. Filo is very simple to use as long as you remember a few rules. It should always be defrosted thoroughly before use. Once exposed to the air, the sheets of pastry dry out and crack. You should cover any sheets you are not using with a damp cloth. When making shells, as in this recipe, the filo can be baked first. When baking a strudel or filled pie, always make the filling first and then prepare the pastry. Brush the sheets with plenty of melted butter, or a mixture of butter and oil. Oil on its own will work but the end result is softer and quite dry.

Tiny button mushrooms are ideal for this dish as they fit well into the delicate filo shells. Add colour by mixing them with one or two other vegetables such as baby corn and diced red pepper. Baby courgettes also work well. Serve these shells as a light lunch dish with a simple green salad and *Baked Italian Tomatoes with Basil and Balsamic Vinegar* (page 93).

SERVES 4

25 g (1 oz) butter plus
extra for greasing
1 tablespoon olive oil
4 sheets filo pastry

For the filling

1 tablespoon oil
2 spring onions, chopped
1 red pepper, de-seeded and
   diced
4 baby sweetcorn, chopped
225 g (8 oz) tiny button
   mushrooms

2 tablespoons chopped fresh
   parsley
Salt and freshly ground black
   pepper
4 tablespoons crème fraîche
2 tablespoons snipped fresh
   chives

Pre-heat the oven to 200°C/400°F/gas 6.

Melt 25 g (1 oz) butter with the oil. Cut each sheet of filo into 4 pieces to line 4 indi-vidual ramekin dishes. Grease the ramekins well. Brush a square of pastry with melted butter and oil on both sides and place in a ramekin. Then add another brushed square at a different angle, overlapping the edge of the ramekin. Continue until each ramekin is lined with 4 squares of filo. Bake the cases for 10 minutes or until crisp and golden. Leave to cool and then remove carefully from the ramekins.

For the filling, heat the oil and fry the spring onions. Then add the pepper, sweetcorn, whole mushrooms and parsley. Cook quickly until just tender. Season well. Divide the vegetables between the shells, then spoon over the crème fraîche. Garnish with the chives. Serve immediately.

Patty Pans

This is my favourite new vegetable. Patty pans are tiny fluted squashes about 2.5 cm (1 inch) in diameter. They come in a pale green or delicate yellow, different colour but same flavour. They have quite a close texture like larger squashes but taste a little more nutty and have no seeds to speak of. You eat the whole lot – and so you should given the price. They are expensive but are worth it for their look.

They are best steamed or microwaved for a few minutes until soft, then served with a sauce.

Patty Pans, Baby Aubergines and Tomatoes with Goat's Cheese Sauce

This recipe is simplicity itself but utterly delicious. I think it could make a smart supper, along with rice or interesting breads, or an elegant first course.

If you haven't got a flavoured oil, infuse a peeled clove of garlic by frying this gently in plain oil first and then removing it from the pan before continuing.

SERVES 4

275 g (10 oz) patty pans
3–4 tablespoons flavoured oil
  (Herb Oil, see page 80, or
  garlic)
275 g (10 oz) baby aubergines
12 cherry tomatoes

For the sauce

25 g (1 oz) butter
100 g (4 oz) soft goat's cheese
100 g (4 oz) fromage frais
1 tablespoon chopped fresh basil leaves
Salt and freshly ground black pepper

Steam, boil or microwave the patty pans until just soft, then drain and set aside.

Heat the oil and cook the aubergines over a gentle heat for about 5–6 minutes, add the patty pans and the cherry tomatoes and cook for a further 3–4 minutes.

To make the sauce, melt the butter and beat in the goat's cheese heating gently until the cheese melts. Add the fromage frais and beat it to make a thick sauce. Add the basil, season to taste and heat through.

Serve the hot vegetables with a coating of sauce.

OVERLEAF
Left: *Miniature Cauliflower with Saffron Sauce* (page 45)
Right: *Baby Vegetables Poached in Fresh Herb Marinade* (page 46)

Root Vegetables

Baby carrots, turnips and parsnips – there are now plastic-wrapped official packets of all these in the supermarkets. They are much more expensive than full-size root vegetables and frankly the difference in flavour doesn't warrant the expense. Better to look for the new season crop and pick out the smallest you can find. I have found a better choice and flavour in the organic produce sold by decent wholefood shops.

Gratin of Winter Baby Vegetables with Cider and Mustard

The accompanying sauce for these baby vegetables is like a fondue with cheese and cider melted together. Serve these as a supper dish with a baked potato. Use a selection of baby parsnips, carrots and leeks.

SERVES 4

900 g–1.25 kg (2–2½ lb) baby vegetables (see above)

For the sauce

25 g (1 oz) butter
225 g (8 oz) strong Cheddar, grated
6 tablespoons strong cider
1 tablespoon prepared mustard
Salt and freshly ground black pepper

Prepare the vegetables by lightly steaming, microwaving or boiling until tender, then keep warm in a flameproof dish.

To make the sauce, melt the butter, then add the grated cheese, cider and mustard, stir well until the cheese has melted and the ingredients blend together. Season to taste. Pour the sauce over the vegetables and put the dish under the grill. Grill until the sauce bubbles and begins to brown.

UNUSUAL AND EXOTIC VEGETABLES

This personal selection of vegetables could just have easily been grouped under the title Curious, Intriguing, Neglected or as Covent Garden would have it 'Queer Gear'. None of these titles have quite the cachet of 'exotic' which I hope will tempt you into this chapter.

Why aren't these vegetables more popular in the first place? One reason might be their size. Is it really worth lugging home two kilos of squash? It could be their skin – the craggy knotted celeriac or dull-looking sweet potato don't draw you in the way that a glowing collection of red and yellow peppers might. Perhaps it all lies in the name. Anything labelled the 'cabbage-turnip' sounds institutional rather than inspirational.

Ah, but what of the flavour and texture inside some of these unpromising vegetables. I think there are some delicious discoveries to make here. The golden butternut squash, the slippery okra, the salty tang of arame, all deserve at least one trip home from the supermarket. Like me, you may find yourself going back for more.

This is only a selection of the weird and wonderful. I've listed the vegetables in alphabetical order followed by a recipe. Some of the vegetables mentioned here also crop up elsewhere in the book.

Butternut Squash

The butternut is one of my favourite of the larger squashes. Its clumsy pear shape and smooth pale skin hide a cheering orange flesh with a good sweet flavour. The outer skin is deceptive, it looks hard, but is in fact quite thin and once cooked, edible.

Just a word or two about the whole squash family. There is an enormous variety in the tribe which divide roughly into summer and winter squashes. Winter squash generally have yellow to orange flesh with a close-grained texture and sweet taste. Summer squash are paler, sometimes green or cream, with not quite such a good flavour. All squash should look well filled out with unblemished skins. If sold in a wedge, the flesh should look firm and not fibrous. Squash will store for several weeks in a cool airy place. It doesn't have to be the fridge.

Most squashes can be plainly served as a side vegetable. The flavour is better if they are baked first rather than boiled. This also saves you looking for a gigantic pan. Split the squash in half. Remove the seeds with a spoon. Place cut side down on a baking tray and cook for 25–45 minutes at 190°C/375°F/gas 5 depending on the size of the squash. Mash with butter or vinaigrette. Chop for casseroles or stir-fry dishes. If the skin is thin it is edible. Squashes with thicker skins can be stuffed, but I find the whole thing rather unwieldy. The exception is the pumpkin. The outer shell makes a splendid tureen which can be filled with, as you would expect, pumpkin soup.

Butternut Squash Soup with Lime and Ginger

Butternut squash with its warm orange colour makes a marvellous soup. Although the outer skin looks indigestible, it will purée to give a smooth texture. Not peeling the squash will save you time and increase the flavour of the finished soup.

SERVES 4

2 tablespoons sunflower oil
1 onion, chopped
1 clove garlic, peeled and crushed
15 g (½ oz) root ginger, peeled and grated
900 g (2 lb) butternut squash, de-seeded (not peeled) and chopped

900 ml (1½ pints) vegetable stock
Juice and zest of 1 lime
Salt and freshly ground black pepper

Heat the oil and gently cook the onion and garlic. Add the ginger and butternut squash and cook slowly in a covered pan for 10 minutes. Add the stock, bring to the boil and simmer for 40 minutes or until the squash is really tender. Cool slightly then liquidize until smooth. Add the juice and zest of 1 lime. Season to taste. Re-heat before serving.

Celeriac

This is a vegetable that is not going to win any beauty competitions with its knobbly shaggy exterior. Celeriac is the swollen stem base of a type of celery. It has the aroma and taste of celery.

Look for medium-sized celeriac. Choose those that are heavy for their size. Large older-looking roots can be woody, or worse still, have a hollow interior. Keep celeriac in a cool place or the fridge.

To cook, trim off all the outer skin. The flesh will discolour very quickly. Chop and use immediately, or keep in water to which you have added a little lemon juice.

Celeriac is fine in casseroles and stews, but I prefer to show it off more as a side vegetable. Sauté in a little butter or oil, soften in wine and then partner it with any of the new soft cheeses – fromage frais and the like.

Celeriac and Emmental Strudel

The nutty flavour of celeriac combines well with Emmental and makes an easy filling for this filo pie. Filo is one of the easiest pastries to work with. For extra guidance, see page 47.

Serve this pie with *Many Mushroom Sauce* (page 32) or *Roasted Garlic Sauce* (page 235).

SERVES 4

25 g (1 oz) butter
450 g (1 lb) celeriac, peeled and diced
2 tablespoons white wine
100 g (4 oz) fromage frais
175 g (6 oz) Emmental, grated
2 eggs, beaten

2 tablespoons chopped fresh parsley
Salt and freshly ground black pepper
8 sheets filo pastry
25 g (1 oz) butter, melted
2 tablespoons olive oil

Melt the butter and gently cook the celeriac until fairly soft. Add the wine and cook for 10 minutes over a gentle heat. Leave to cool slightly then purée the mixture with the fromage frais. Mix in the Emmental, beaten eggs and parsley and season to taste.

Pre-heat the oven to 200°C/400°F/gas 6.

To prepare the pie, brush a sheet of filo with a mixture of melted butter and olive oil and place in an ovenproof dish 20 × 20 cm (8 × 8 inches). Add 3 more brushed sheets in the same way. Cover with celeriac filling and then put on the remaining sheets of filo brushing well with melted butter. Cut a cross through the pastry to the bottom of the dish. Bake for 25–30 minutes or until the pastry is cooked. Serve hot.

Jerusalem Artichokes

I can't help but boast about the success and the fun my four-year-old and I have had growing these. We planted half a dozen tubers in front of the kitchen window. Only then did we find out they were likely to grow to 2 metres high. And so they did. Despite the jungle outlook from inside, it was great watching them grow and then having the joy of harvesting. The six originals had magically multiplied yielding a good crop.

The drawback to Jerusalem artichokes is their preparation. Their knobbly surface needs scrubbing well and then careful peeling. If you have grown them, you can be more ruthless about what you discard. Certain commercially grown Jerusalem artichokes have smoother skins and you should certainly pick these when buying them. Keep Jerusalem artichokes, as with other root vegetables, in a cool, dry place, or the fridge.

The Jerusalem artichoke, which bears no relation to the globe artichoke, has a nutty flavour with a pale crisp flesh. Like celeriac it discolours quickly, so once chopped use straightaway or keep in acidulated water. Jerusalem artichokes make marvellous creamy soups, but you can also roast or fry them like a potato.

Jerusalem Artichokes
in Cream and Mustard Sauce

This cream and wine sauce is spiked with mustard. It is good with a variety of vegetables but a perfect foil for artichokes. I could make a meal of this, but it is strictly a side vegetable.

SERVES 4

450 g (1 lb) Jerusalem artichokes	*225 g (8 oz) crème fraîche*
25 g (1 oz) butter	*1 teaspoon Dijon mustard*
1 tablespoon olive oil	*Salt and freshly ground black*
2 shallots, finely diced	*pepper*
120 ml (4 fl oz) white wine	

Scrub the artichokes and thinly peel if necessary. Chop roughly and boil in water for 15–20 minutes or until just tender. Drain and set aside.

Melt the butter with the oil and gently cook the shallots until translucent, toss in the cooked artichokes and fry until just beginning to brown. Remove from the pan and transfer to an ovenproof dish and keep warm. Pour the wine into the saucepan and bring to the boil, simmer for 4 minutes to reduce, then add the crème fraîche and mustard and stir to make a smooth sauce. Cook until heated through and season to taste. Pour over the warm artichokes and serve immediately.

Kohlrabi

Kohlrabi is the thickened stem of a variety of cabbage. Roughly the size of a golf ball (and that is the size you should aim to buy), it has a purple or green skin marked with distinstive slashes where the leaf stalks have been removed. The flesh is white, the flavour hot and peppery, similar to a young turnip or a white cabbage.

To prepare, simply trim the kohlrabi and scrub rather than peel. Grate a small amount raw into salads to add a hot taste. Cooked, it blends well with most vegetable combinations. For a plain side vegetable, I prefer to steam or microwave as this gives the best flavour.

Roasted Kohlrabi with Almonds

If I'm using kohlrabi, I like an opportunity to show it off. Roasted kohlrabi is distinctive. It pairs well, colour- and flavour-wise with butternut squash.

SERVES 4

275 g (10 oz) kohlrabi, scrubbed and cubed
275 g (10 oz) butternut squash, de-seeded and cubed
8 shallots, peeled
3–4 tablespoons olive oil

Salt and freshly ground black pepper
2 tablespoons whole blanched almonds
1 tablespoon shoyu

Pre-heat the oven to 200°C/400°F/gas 6.

Steam all the vegetables for 5 minutes or until just soft. Toss them in the oil, adding seasoning. Place in a roasting dish in one layer and bake for 15 minutes or until tender.

On a separate baking sheet, lightly toast the almonds for 4–5 minutes.

Once the kohlrabi is tender, toss the vegetables in the shoyu, place them in a serving dish and top with the almonds. Serve hot.

Okra

Okra or ladies' fingers are a distinctive five-sided vegetable. They are green and about the length of a fine bean, or indeed finger. When cooked they yield slippery smooth juices that add a distinctive quality to a stew or sauce as well as thickening it slightly. American dishes containing okra are called gumbo, which nicely conjures up a gluey image (see *Sweet Potato Gumbo* on page 65). Okra is not used exclusively in the States, it is an important ingredient in African and Middle Eastern cuisines as well as in Indian cookery where they are known as bhindi.

To prepare okra, buy fresh-looking specimens which should be firm not floppy. Remove the conical ends.

Spiced Okra and Potato

This is an interesting dish where the vegetables are coated in a spiced nutty flour as they cook. Gram flour should be availabe in larger supermarkets or specialist healthfood shops. Asafoetida, also known as Heeng, is an extremely pungent spice that is used in very small quantities in many Indian recipes. It is not usually stocked by supermarkets but should be available in Indian shops. It can be bought in lump or powder form, the former is supposed to keep longer but both will keep some time. Wrap it carefully in polythene to contain the smell. For more information on the spices see pages 153–6.

SERVES 4

4–6 tablespoons sunflower oil
225 g (8 oz) okra, chopped
275 g (10 oz) potato, peeled and chopped
1 red pepper, de-seeded and diced
50 g (2 oz) gram flour
2 tablespoons desiccated coconut
25 g (1 oz) unsalted peanuts, ground
¼ teaspoon asafoetida
½ teaspoon paprika
¼ teaspoon turmeric
¼ teaspoon salt
Juice of ½ lemon

Heat the oil and gently cook the okra, potato and pepper, stirring frequently.

Mix together the gram flour, coconut, peanuts, spices and salt. Sprinkle this mixture over the slightly softened vegetables. Mix well. Cover the pan. Cook over a very gentle heat for 35–40 minutes, stirring frequently.

Pour over the lemon juice and adjust the seasoning. Serve hot.

Red Cabbage

Red cabbage is a great winter vegetable. Close in texture like the Dutch white cabbage, it is best shredded. There is very little waste. You only need to discard the outer leaves if they are blemished or discoloured. Red cabbage will keep for some time in a cool place. If you only use half at a time, wrap the rest in cling film and keep it in the fridge.

Red cabbage is one of the few vegetables I can think of that genuinely benefits from lengthy cooking. Shredded and gently stewed with apples, sultanas and spices, it can be served hot or cold. Make a large amount and freeze it. It comes in useful as a side vegetable.

Sea Vegetables

Sea vegetables or, as they are more charmingly named 'sea greens', are increasingly available in health and wholefood shops. Whilst I could write at length on the merits of eating them (rich sources of minerals, help to eliminate toxins, high in protein), I also recognize that it is very difficult to look at seaweed and think 'yummy! food!'.

Seaweed is a good deal better than it was. When I first sold it in my shop some fifteen years ago, it needed hours of simmering and was very tough. The Japanese seaweeds available today need brief soaking, little cooking and have a pleasant salty tang. With the exception of nori (see page 143), they are best mixed with other vegetables, used almost like a herb to season and flavour. Here are a few details on some of the most popular sea vegetables.

Arame

Arame grows in delicate black fronds which are very appealing. These are so fine that it is not always necessary to soak them. Arame goes well with sweeter vegetables such as peppers. It has a tender texture and mild salty taste.

Dulse

Dulse has purple reddish fronds with a slightly spicy flavour. I think it goes well with red and green cabbage and also works well in soups and stews.

Hijiki

This is similar to arame but thicker and stronger in flavour.

Kombu

Kombu comprises fairly wide stems, black in colour. It is used as a flavouring in soups and stocks. Use a strip a couple of inches long and remove after cooking as you would a bay leaf.

Wakame

This seaweed has a mild flavour and can be soaked and mixed with vegetables. It can also be toasted and crumbled as a condiment.

Red Cabbage and Arame Sauté with Orange and Sesame

Recently I've discovered that red cabbage also works well in a semi stir-fry where it is cooked for about 10 minutes overall. Its strong sweet nutty flavour pairs well with one of my favourite sea vegetables, arame (see page 60).

SERVES 4

25 g (1 oz) arame or hijiki
450 g (1 lb) red cabbage
2 tablespoons sunflower oil
6 tablespoons fresh orange juice
2 tablespoons toasted sesame oil
1 tablespoon balsamic vinegar
2 cloves garlic, peeled and
    crushed
1 tablespoon shoyu
Salt and freshly ground black
    pepper

Soak the arame or hijiki in hot water for 15 minutes then drain well. Shred the red cabbage finely.

Heat the oil and cook the cabbage and arame for 3–4 minutes. Mix all the remaining ingredients together and season to taste. Pour the mixture over the cabbage, stir briefly then cover. Cook on a low heat for 5–6 minutes or until the cabbage is just soft. Serve immediately.

OVERLEAF
Right: *Red Cabbage and Arame Sauté
with Orange and Sesame*
Left: *Butternut Squash Soup
with Lime and Ginger* (page 54)

Spaghetti Squash

Just have fun with this vegetable. It does live up to its name. The flesh once cooked lifts up in strands and is quite spaghetti-ish. What I particularly like is its crisp texture.

Baked Spaghetti Squash

SERVES 4

1 large spaghetti squash (about
900 g–1.5 kg/2–3 lb)
50 g (2 oz) butter
2 tablespoons freshly grated
Parmesan
Salt and freshly ground black
pepper

Pre-heat the oven to 190°C/375°F/gas 5.

Cut the squash in half lengthways. Remove the seeds with a spoon. Place cut side down on a large baking sheet. Bake for 30 minutes or until quite tender.

Dot each half with butter and sprinkle with Parmesan, salt and pepper. Serve hot.

Sweet Potato

With new regulations to curb the bendyness of a banana, I wonder what bureaucrats will ever do with the sweet potato. This tuber comes in a great variety of shapes and sizes. Its skin may be smooth or ribbed and the flesh ranges from white to deep orange or purple.

Pale-coloured varieties have a more floury texture with a chestnut flavour. The yellow and orange ones are sweeter with a softer, more watery flesh. To check what you are buying, scratch the skin.

Sweet potatoes should be scrubbed rather than peeled. They can be treated like the ordinary potato, baked, boiled, roasted or mashed. I prefer the more nutty flavoured varieties as side vegetables and use the more brightly coloured ones to cheer up a mixture in a stew.

Sweet Potato Gumbo

Gumbo is the name of a stew from the American South. It can be made from many different vegetables but usually contains okra which gives it its characteristic texture. When first cooked, okra appears rather slimy, but it will gradually thicken a mixture and help blend flavours together. Serve this stew with *Quesadillas with Roasted Tomatoes* (page 109).

SERVES 4

2 tablespoons sunflower oil
1 onion, chopped
1 clove garlic, peeled and crushed
100 g (4 oz) okra, chopped
100 g (4 oz) baby sweetcorn, chopped
225 g (8 oz) button mushrooms
450 g (1 lb) sweet potato, peeled and diced

1 tablespoon chopped sun-dried tomatoes (in oil)
550 g (1¼ lb) passata (page 124)
1 teaspoon chopped fresh marjoram
1 teaspoon chopped fresh thyme
1 teaspoon paprika
Salt and freshly ground black pepper

Heat the oil then add the onion and garlic and cook until soft. Next add the vegetables and cook for 5–7 minutes or until just beginning to soften. Add the sun-dried tomatoes, passata, herbs and paprika. If necessary add a little liquid but the stew should not be too sloppy. Bring to the boil and cook for 50–60 minutes or until all the ingredients are very soft. Season to taste.

SALAD LEAVES

Leaf salads have blossomed. Colours range from green through to red and purple, textures from crisp to soft. Whilst a bowl of salad leaves won't fill you up, their freshness brightens up any meal.

Buying and Storing Salad Leaves

Pre-packed salad mixtures have popularized an enormous variety of leaves. These mixes are expensive but there is no waste as the ingredients are ready trimmed and washed. I think some freshness is lost, particularly with leaves that are ready torn. Live lettuces are a new addition to the salad section. Rather like growing herbs, these miniature lettuces are in small pots. The idea is that you can remove outer leaves and the plant will continue to grow and therefore be fresh. I tried a mixed selection which was very successful but expensive.

Whether you buy a pre-pack or several whole salad items, always buy from a supplier whose turnover is quick. Never get anything that looks tired. Remove any tight polythene packaging as soon as possible. Store in a loose-fitting polythene bag and keep the leaves in the fridge. Before use, clean whole salad items thoroughly. Wash gently under cold running water and dry in a salad spinner or basket.

Using Salad Leaves

I like the convenience of ready-made (and cleaned) salad leaves but some of the mixes can be dull or swamped with one ingredient. To help you make your own concoctions, the following is a quick guide to salad leaves, noting colour, texture and flavour, so you can take it in at a glance. Then I've given a couple of recipes for varying salads made from leaves. Following these are some recipes for slightly more substantial salads using a particular type of leaf.

For other salads look in the chapter on oils where I've concentrated on dressings.

Butterhead lettuce: soft green leaves with a mild flavour.
Belgian chicory: pale leaves are tightly bunched together to make a pointed shoot or chicon. Clean bitter taste. Good crisp texture.
Chinese leaves: pale green with white mid-ribs. Crisp, delicate.

Cos lettuce: large-leafed, crisp and refreshing.

Corn salad (or lamb's lettuce, mâche): rosettes of soft small leaves, muted green. Mild taste.

Endive (or frisée): curly jagged bright green to yellow leaves. Bitter flavour, crisp texture.

Iceberg: pale and very crisp. Tends to have little flavour.

Little Gem: smaller version of cos. Pale to bright green leaves. Crisp with sweet flavour.

Lollo rosso: (also comes in green called **Lollo biondo**) very curled, beautiful Italian lettuce. Delicate, mild flavour.

Oakleaf: green and red varieties. The red variety has a maroon edge with a dark almost olive-green interior. Strong flavour.

Radicchio: strong red colour ribbed with white. Crisp. Tangy.

Rocket: related to the mustard family. The young notched leaves have a warm, peppery flavour.

Sorrel: bright green, slender leaves that have a sharp lemony tang with a hint of pepper.

Spinach: choose baby spinach. Dark green soft leaves with sharp taste.

Here are two salad leaves that are virtually impossible to buy but you may grow or find wild:

Dandelion: wild dandelion is very bitter, the cultivated varieties are much milder in flavour.

Purslane: pretty leaf rosettes. Soft texture and clean taste.

Dark Green Salad with Rough Tapenade Dressing

This highly flavoured dark dressing works best with strongly flavoured salad leaves such as oakleaf lettuce, baby spinach, radicchio and watercress.

SERVES 4

For the dressing

10 green olives, pitted
1–2 tablespoons capers
1 clove garlic, peeled
Juice and zest of 1 lemon
3–4 tablespoons olive oil or
  Herb Oil (see page 80)

1 teaspoon chopped fresh
  thyme
1 teaspoon chopped fresh
  oregano
Salt and freshly ground black
  pepper

75–100 g (3–4 oz) mixed salad
leaves (see page 67)

Roughly chop the olives, capers and garlic. Mix together with the lemon juice and zest, olive oil and herbs. Leave to stand for 15 minutes or so for the flavours to infuse. Then season to taste and add more oil if you prefer.

Clean the salad leaves if necessary and mix together in a bowl. Toss in the dressing and serve immediately.

Herb and Leaf Salad

Use a variety of salad leaves with herbs to make a very fresh, interesting green salad. It needs minimal dressing – I think just a little oil. If you have nasturtiums in the garden, they are ideal. There are other edible flowers, for example pansy, primrose, daisy, chive flowers and borage. You may find some larger supermarkets sell salad flowers.

I think flowers add a finishing touch but if you have none, keep back a few sprigs of herbs to decorate the bowl.

SERVES 4

75 g (3 oz) mixed salad leaves
  (such as lollo rosso,
  butterhead lettuce, baby
  spinach)
25 g (1 oz) sprigs of mixed fresh
  herbs (such as parsley,
  chervil, dill, thyme, sorrel,
  tarragon)

1–2 tablespoons best-quality
  olive oil
4–6 nasturtium flowers

Clean and prepare the salad leaves and herbs and place them in a bowl. Just before serving drizzle over the olive oil. Garnish with nasturtium flowers and serve immediately.

Chicory in Crème Fraîche
with Horseradish and Mustard

Chicory is characterized by its bitter taste. The white pointed heads of
Belgian chicory are only slightly bitter and they do have a splendid
crunchy texture ideal for eating raw.

SERVES 4

For the dressing

100 g (4 oz) crème fraîche
½ teaspoon creamed horseradish
½ teaspoon prepared mustard
Salt and freshly ground black
  pepper

2 head chicory
Lollo rosso leaves
Watercress

Make the dressing by mixing all the ingredients together. Chop the chicory and mix in
the dressing.

Line a bowl with lollo rosso and watercress and pile the salad into the centre.

Crisp Lettuce
with Strawberry and Mint Vinaigrette

Strawberries and cucumber go well together and have a natural affinity
with mint. If you can get a strawberry vinegar for the dressing this will
accentuate the flavour, otherwise use a white wine vinegar or balsamic
vinegar for a slightly sweeter taste.

OVERLEAF
Left: *Roast Peppers with Walnut Vinaigrette*
and Sorrel (page 74)
Right: *Crisp Lettuce with Strawberry and*
Mint Vinaigrette

SERVES 4

For the vinaigrette

3 tablespoons sunflower oil
1 tablespoon strawberry vinegar
(see page 69)
2–3 tablespoons chopped fresh
mint

1 teaspoon concentrated apple
or apple and strawberry
juice
Salt and freshly ground black
pepper

For the salad

1 × 10 cm (4 inch) piece
cucumber, peeled
12 strawberries

1 crisp green apple
1 cos lettuce
Mint sprigs to garnish

Mix all the ingredients for the vinaigrette together and season to taste.

Chop the cucumber, slice the strawberries and dice the apple. Toss in the vinaigrette.

Wash and dry the lettuce. Arrange the leaves in a bowl and pile the salad on top. Garnish with mint leaves.

Quickly Wilted Leaves in Warm Hazelnut Dressing

Roasted hazelnuts and garlic are gently heated in oil to make this warm dressing with its subtle undertone. This type of warm salad must be served immediately so that the leafy ingredients are just beginning to wilt and not at the stage of looking sorry for themselves.

SERVES 4

75 g (3 oz) mixed salad leaves
(such as baby spinach, corn
salad, lollo rosso and endive)
15 g (½ oz) hazelnuts
50 g (2 oz) fine beans, trimmed
50 g (2 oz) button mushrooms
2 tablespoons olive oil

1 clove garlic, peeled and
chopped
2 tablespoons hazelnut oil
1 teaspoon white wine vinegar
Salt and freshly ground black
pepper

Pre-heat the oven to 200°C/400°F/gas 6.

Prepare the salad leaves and divide between 4 medium plates.

Place the hazelnuts on a baking tray and roast for 3–4 minutes. Leave to cool, then rub off the skins and chop coarsely but quite evenly.

Blanch the fine beans in boiling water for 2–3 minutes, drain and refresh. Slice the mushrooms.

Heat the olive oil and, over a low heat, fry the garlic, without letting it colour. Add the roasted hazelnut pieces and cook for 2–3 minutes. Off the heat, stir in the hazelnut oil and wine vinegar and season to taste.

Arrange the warm beans and mushroom slices over the salad leaves, drizzle over the warm dressing and serve immediately.

Roast Aubergine Salad with Baby Spinach

Aubergine usually features in cooked salad mixtures such as caponata. I think it comes into its own when roasted and marinated. The end result is a hearty salad that could be a starter or part of a main course salad platter with focaccia, *Spiced Sesame and Shoyu Dip* (page 162), hummus and *Marinated Olives* (page 78). If you can't get kumquats, use fresh orange zest as a garnish.

SERVES 4

2 large aubergines
1 tablespoon Chilli Oil (see
page 80)

For the dressing

2 tablespoons sesame oil
3 chopped spring onions
2 cloves garlic, peeled and finely chopped

2 tablespoons shoyu
1 small green chilli, de-seeded and diced
Juice and zest of 1 small orange

50–75 g (2–3 oz) baby spinach leaves
6–8 kumquats, sliced

Pre-heat the oven to 200°C/400°F/gas 6.

Slice the aubergines lengthwise and brush with chilli oil. Place on a baking tray and bake for 12 minutes. Mix all the dressing ingredients together. Place the aubergine slices in a large dish and cover with the dressing. Leave for 2 hours, turning the pieces over occasionally.

To assemble the salad, line a large plate with baby spinach, arrange the aubergine slices on top and pour over some of the dressing. Garnish with slices of kumquat.

Roast Peppers
with Walnut Vinaigrette and Sorrel

Roast peppers are entirely different from raw peppers. They have a melting juicy texture and blend well with vinaigrette dressings. They are easy to roast. Just put them in a hot oven until the skin blackens. It should then come off easily. Once roasted, peppers will keep for several days in the refrigerator. This salad is rich in oils and I like to balance that with a sharp-flavoured salad leaf such as sorrel or rocket.

SERVES 4

2 red peppers
2 yellow peppers
Olive oil for brushing
2–3 tablespoons Toasted Walnut
    Vinaigrette (page 87)

Salt and freshly ground black
    pepper
25 g (1 oz) walnut pieces
5–6 sorrel or rocket leaves,
    roughly torn

Pre-heat the oven to 200°C/400°F/gas 6.

Cut the peppers in half. Remove the seeds and white pith. Brush the outer surface with olive oil then place the halves on a baking tray. Bake for 40–50 minutes or until the skin is well charred. Remove from the oven, leave to cool a little then peel off the skin. Use a knife if necessary. Slice the pepper into thin strips and toss in 2 tablespoons walnut vinaigrette. Make sure the pieces are well coated. Adjust the seasoning if necessary.

Toast the walnuts for 3–5 minutes in the oven, cool and chop roughly. Arrange the sorrel or rocket on large plate, cover with pepper mixture, then sprinkle over the walnut pieces. Serve at room temperature.

OILS, AROMATIC OILS AND VINEGARS

I once splashed out on some estate-bottled olive oil which was more expensive than good champagne. It was worth it. Rich in colour, it had a smooth after-taste with an elusive mixture of pepper, herbs and fruit. It became a treasured possession, measured out in thimblefuls and then, sometimes, I would shut my eyes and pour away happily.

For fun I gave a similar bottle away for Christmas, resisting the temptation to say 'this will be the most expensive oil you have tasted'. The thank you for this present was just a gasp of astonishment at the heady flavour. By the way, if you discover a gem, remember that, like wine, estate-bottled oils will vary from year to year. I don't use these extravagent oils every day. For general use, I have two oils, a good-quality virgin olive and a sunflower oil. For flavouring I have a walnut, a hazelnut and a toasted sesame oil. I've given details of these with appropriate recipes within this chapter.

Buying and Storing Oil
There are a bewildering range of culinary oils on sale today from palest gold through to amber, rich green and brown. Supermarkets are offering an increasing choice, especially with olive oil. Wholefood shops tend to sell unrefined or cold pressed versions of basic oils such as sunflower oil. These oils have not been subjected to any more processing than is needed to extract the oil from the nut or seed. Consequently they often have a stronger taste and smell. It is worth trying a delicatessen or oriental shop for sesame and other nut oils.

Heat and light can oxidize oil causing it to smell sour and taste rancid. To avoid this, oils are best stored in cool dry places, away from sunlight. This might seem impossible advice for cooking oils as you need them to be handy near the cooker. If you are using an oil up fairly quickly, it shouldn't become rancid, but do follow the rules with more precious oils which you won't use so frequently.

If kept in a refrigerator oils will congeal and then need time to warm up before you can mix them properly into dressings.

Vinegars

There are now a good range of vinegars available. For everyday use, I keep a red and a white wine vinegar as well as a cider vinegar. I use these for dressings, vinaigrette and salsa, varying my choice depending on the colour of the finished dressing as well as the other ingredients. Occasionally a fruity vinegar takes my fancy such as blackberry or raspberry. These are interchangeable with the basic vinegars but are useful for highlighting a particular flavour. The same applies to herb vinegars. Rice wine vinegar is mild and delicate with a clean taste and goes well with oriental dishes in particular.

Sherry vinegar falls into a different category. It is almost sweet, mellow and aromatic. I use it sprinkled over vegetables as a seasoning. Try it with buttered sauté mushrooms. Delicious. For more on Balsamic vinegar see page 93.

One plus point about having numerous vinegars is that they do keep for a reasonable length of time. However, I would advise buying small quantities of unusual types.

Olive Oil

The versatility of olive oil makes it ideal for all sorts of culinary purposes. It heats well for frying and cooking, and tastes good enough to mix into dressings and dips.

Estate-bottled olive oil has to be set aside from the general discussion because its price instantly puts it in the luxury category. This olive oil is made from olives grown on one estate and therefore, like wine from particular vineyards, has a unique flavour. This oil should be used unadulterated on dishes where the flavour will shine through.

For mere mortals, there is still plenty of choice! Olive oil is commonly categorized as virgin, extra virgin, and pure. Virgin olive oil has not been heated or chemically processed. It is also graded according to its acidity, the highest grade has the lowest acidity and is therefore the best oil. This is known as extra virgin. Virgin olive oil is slightly more acidic. The cheapest olive oil is 'pure' olive oil, which is a mixture of virgin oil and some olive oil that has been refined.

Apart from processing, the country of origin and the subsequent blending will influence the flavour and colour of the finished olive oil. Personally, I am not loyal to one brand, but change frequently to get a subtle variety of tastes.

Tabbouleh

A good-quality olive oil with peppery or herbal undertones adds to the overall flavour of this classic salad. I think Tabbouleh goes with virtually any leafy salad. Serve it with flans such as *Caramelized Onion Tart* (page 208) or filo dishes such as *Baby Vegetables in Filo Shells with Crème Fraîche* (page 47). It is also a useful substantial salad to include on a Mezze table (see page 198)

SERVES 4

100 g (4 oz) bulgar wheat
A pinch of salt
150 ml (5 fl oz) boiling water
4 tablespoons chopped fresh
    parsley

2 tablespoons chopped fresh
    coriander
2 tablespoons chopped fresh
    mint

For the dressing

50 ml (2 fl oz) good-quality
    virgin olive oil
50 ml (2 fl oz) lemon
    juice

2–3 cloves garlic, peeled and
    crushed
Salt and freshly ground black
    pepper

Mix the bulgar wheat with the salt and pour over the boiling water. Leave to stand for about 15 minutes. Put the bulgar wheat in a fine sieve and press lightly to get rid of all excess moisture. Stir in the fresh herbs.

Mix the olive oil with the lemon juice and garlic. Season well. Mix the dressing gently into the bulgar wheat. Adjust the seasoning.

Marinated Olives

*1 tablespoon dried oregano or
  marjoram
2 teaspoons dried thyme
2 bay leaves, crumbled*

*Enough unpitted black olives to
  fill a 300 ml (10 fl oz)
  preserving jar
Olive oil*

Mix all the herbs together. Pack a layer of olives in the bottom of the cleaned, preferably sterilized, jar, then add a scattering of herbs. Pack in some more olives and more herbs and continue layering like this until the jar is full. Then pour enough olive oil in to fill the jar completely.

Leave for at least a week. Once opened, store in a cool place.

Marinated Feta
with Sun-dried Tomatoes

In this marinade the oil is heated with the herbs to draw out their flavours. Serve the cheese in bowls along with *Marinated Olives* (above) and *Baby Vegetables Poached in Fresh Herb Marinade* (see page 46), or with crisp cos lettuce, cucumber and chopped spring onions. This dish is ideal as part of a salad meal, or can be offered as a snack.

SERVES 4

*250 ml (8 fl oz) olive oil
1 teaspoon black peppercorns,
  lightly crushed
3 sprigs of rosemary
3 sprigs of thyme
2 bay leaves*

*3 cloves garlic, peeled and
  crushed
150 g (5 oz) feta cheese
2–3 sun-dried tomatoes (in oil),
  thinly sliced*

Heat the oil with the pepper, herbs and garlic. Infuse the mixture for about 5 minutes, keeping the oil fairly hot.

Cut the Feta into cubes. Put into a heatproof dish in a single layer with the sun-dried tomato strips. Pour the hot oil over the cheese and leave to cool.

Pack everything into a clean, preferably sterilized, jar and store in the refrigerator. Use within a week.

Grilled Artichoke Salad
with Broccoli and Peppercorn Mayonnaise

I buy chargrilled marinated artichokes which, although expensive, are truly worth it for a special treat. With them I make this simple salad starter.

You can buy a ready-made mixture of five peppers (black, white, pink, green and pimento) which is ideal for this dish. Alternatively mix separate quantities of pink, green and black. When crushed, the colourful particles look gorgeous in mayonnaise adding texture and bite.

SERVES 4

*4–6 chargrilled marinated
    artichoke hearts
225 g (8 oz) broccoli florets
3–4 teaspoons mixed
    peppercorns
4–6 tablespoons mayonnaise or
    mayonnaise and plain
    yoghurt
Salt
25–50 g (1–2 oz) mixed salad
    leaves*

Drain the artichokes of oil. Slice in half. Steam the broccoli florets until just tender. Drain and refresh under cold water.

Crush the peppercorns and mix with the mayonnaise or mayonnaise and yoghurt. Season to taste with salt. Clean and prepare the salad leaves if necessary and arrange them on a platter, cover with artichokes and broccoli and spoon a good quantity of the peppercorn mayonnaise over the top.

Flavoured Oils

Flavoured oils are very simple to make yourself. I think you get the best results using olive oil with its strong colour and aromatic undertones. To infuse oil with whatever flavouring you have chosen, you must have a clean, preferably sterilized, bottle with a cork or screw-top, and patience. It takes a week or so for the flavours to develop.

Use flavoured oils unadulterated where they will be noticed, such as over freshly steamed or grilled vegetables. Herb oils are marvellous in salads, alone or as part of the dressing.

You can use all manner of flavourings and ingredients for marinating in oil whether you want to produce a hot spicy concoction or pungent mixtures redolent with herbs. Whatever you use should be of the best quality, and not blemished, damaged or bruised or it may spoil despite being preserved in oil. Use a good-quality olive oil as this will add to the final result. You can use the resulting flavoured oil for salads, pasta or pizza.

Chilli Oil

This fiery oil is great over cooked vegetables. Substitute it instead of plain oil in recipes which need extra hotness.

MAKES 550 ml (18 fl oz)

550 ml (18 fl oz) olive oil　　　　*3 red or green chillies*
4 cloves garlic, peeled　　　　　*6 black peppercorns*
6 cloves

Place all the ingredients in a clean, preferably sterilized, bottle. Seal with a cork or screw-top and leave for at least 2 weeks. Once the spices are no longer covered by the oil, use up within 10 days.

Herb Oil

MAKES 550 ml (18 fl oz)

550 ml (18 fl oz) olive oil　　　　*Sprigs of thyme, marjoram,*
2 bay leaves　　　　　　　　　　*oregano and parsley*
4 cloves garlic, peeled

Place all the ingredients in a clean, preferably sterilized, bottle. Seal with a cork or screw-top and leave for at least 2 weeks.

Basil Oil

The soft leaves of basil tend to become slimy if preserved whole. Chop and pound them first. I like the flecks of green in the oil but it can be strained if you prefer.

MAKES 250 ml (8 fl oz)

2–3 tablespoons chopped fresh
   basil
250 ml (8 fl oz) olive oil

Chop the basil and pound it in a pestle and mortar. Place the herbs and oil in a clean, preferably sterilized, bottle. Seal with a cork or screw-top and leave for at least 2 weeks, shaking the bottle gently every time you remember.

Cashew Stir-fry in Chilli Oil

This simple stir-fry uses chilli oil to add a lively kick to the nuts and vegetables. Serve this with rice or bulgar wheat.

SERVES 3–4

2–3 tablespoons Chilli Oil
   (see page 80)
175 g (6 oz) cashew pieces
1 onion, chopped
1 clove garlic, peeled and
   crushed
2 sticks celery, diced

1 yellow pepper, de-seeded and
   cut in fine strips
225 g (8 oz) courgettes, diced
225 g (8 oz) mushrooms, sliced
2–3 tablespoons shoyu
2–3 tablespoons lemon juice
Freshly ground black pepper

Heat the oil and fry the cashew pieces until lightly browned. Add the onion and garlic and continue cooking until quite soft. Then add the celery, peppers, courgettes and mushrooms and fry over a high heat until they just begin to soften. Quickly pour on the shoyu and lemon juice, stir well, then cover the pan and cook for 2 minutes or until the liquid has evaporated and the vegetables are just tender. Serve immediately with a little black pepper.

OVERLEAF
Left: *Grilled Artichoke Salad with Broccoli and*
Peppercorn Mayonnaise (page 79)
Right: *Roasted Cashew and Beansprout Salad*
with Salted Lime Dressing (page 92)

Marinated Mushrooms
with Lemon and Green Peppercorns

These marinated mushrooms have a zesty lemon flavour. Make this recipe at least a day before you need it. They should keep for a few days in the fridge. Use these mushrooms along with olives and Feta cheese as snacks before a main meal or as part of a buffet spread.

SERVES 4

450 g (1 lb) button mushrooms
Juice and zest of 1 lemon
150 ml (5 fl oz) Herb Oil
  (see page 80) or olive oil
2 tablespoons white wine
  vinegar

1 bay leaf
1 teaspoon green peppercorns in
  brine, drained and crushed
1 teaspoon fresh thyme
Salt and freshly ground black
  pepper

Wipe the whole mushrooms and put them in a medium saucepan. Cover with water and add the lemon juice and zest. Bring to the boil and cook for 5 minutes. Drain well.

Mix the remaining ingredients in a small pan and heat until it is quite hot. Pour the mixture over the mushrooms and leave overnight. Season to taste.

Nut Oils

Treat these oils as flavourings rather than oils for cooking. Not only are they prohibitively expensive for general use but their flavours, whilst powerful, are lost when heated to any degree. The best way to savour these oils is to use them solo over fresh vegetables or to mix them into dips, dressings and vinaigrettes. Cooked into cakes and pastries their flavour is hard to detect.

Nut oils are made from roasted nuts which are then pressed to release their flavour. The colour of the final oil will depend on the degree of toasting. As with most oil, various grades are available. It is worth shopping around and possibly trying several varieties to find those with the best flavour.

In this chapter I've focused on the two oils most valuable in savoury cooking – hazelnut and walnut oil. However, there's no reason not to make an oil from any nut. Most have a high fat content. The problem is stopping the oil becoming rancid. Other nut oils, such as pine kernel or pistachio are also available.

Hazelnut Oil

Gold or deep gold in colour with the strong scent of the hazelnut, this oil is surprisingly sweet to taste. A few drops are excellent on a plain green salad. When using the oil more generously, I find you don't need quite such an intense flavour to get a good effect. Mix hazelnut oil with another oil and the flavour will still be apparent.

Globe Artichokes
with Roasted Hazelnut Mayonnaise

Roasted hazelnuts taste quite different from plain nuts. I generally have to roast more than I need as I can't help nibbling them as soon as they are cool enough. Added to a hazelnut mayonnaise, they make a good, textured dressing for the artichokes.

SERVES 4

For the mayonnaise

25 g (1 oz) shelled hazelnuts
4 cloves garlic
1 egg
1 tablespoon white wine vinegar

85 ml (3 fl oz) hazelnut oil
85 ml (3 fl oz) sunflower oil
Salt and freshly ground black
   pepper

4 globe artichokes

Pre-heat the oven to 200°C/400°F/gas 6.

Place the hazelnuts on a baking tray and roast them for 5 minutes. Rub off the skins and chop finely.

Roast the whole, unpeeled cloves of garlic for 5 minutes. Then peel and grind them in a food processor. Add the egg and wine vinegar and process for 30 seconds. Gradually add the oils while the machine is still running. Thin the mayonnaise down with extra vinegar if necessary. Season to taste. Stir in the chopped nuts.

To cook the artichokes, trim off the stalks and any discoloured leaves. Boil in a large pan of salted water for 20 minutes or until the lower leaves will pull out fairly easily.

Drain, then serve the artichokes with the mayonnaise in a small dish on the side.

Hazelnut, Egg and Asparagus Salad

Roasted hazelnuts complement the nutty flavour of asparagus. Hazelnut
oil and orange juice are natural partners in this sweet dressing.
Serve this salad as a side dish.

SERVES 4

350 g (12 oz) asparagus
2 eggs
25 g (1 oz) shelled hazelnuts
1 butterhead lettuce

For the vinaigrette

2 tablespoons fresh orange juice	*1 tablespoon cider vinegar*
Zest of ½ orange	*½ teaspoon Dijon mustard*
1 tablespoon sunflower oil	*Salt and freshly ground black*
1 tablespoon hazelnut oil	* pepper*

Trim, then steam or boil the asparagus until tender. Drain and refresh with cold water.
Hard-boil the eggs. Cool. Shell them and remove yolks. Set them to one side and chop
the egg whites finely. Pre-heat the oven to 200°C/400°F/gas 6 and roast the hazelnuts on
a baking tray for 6 minutes. Cool and rub off the skins by rubbing several nuts at a time
in your hands. Chop roughly.

Wash and dry the lettuce. Arrange in a bowl. For the vinaigrette, mix all its ingredients
together then mash in the hard-boiled egg yolks. Season to taste. Toss the salad ingredients and roasted hazelnuts in the vinaigrette. Pile on top of the lettuce and serve.

Walnut Oil

As you would expect, this is a richly flavoured oil and often a bronze gold colour. As
with hazelnut oil you can mix walnut oil with other oils and still get a strong flavour. I
find walnut oil and olive oil make a good pairing.

Walnuts are notorious for going rancid and, as a result, I'm doubly cautious over
walnut oil. Do try and remember to keep it out of a hot kitchen.

Toasted Walnut Vinaigrette

This heavily textured nutty vinaigrette is one of my favourite uses for walnut oil. It keeps well, but will separate slightly. Use it on less than delicate salads, over chunky vegetables, with cheese or as part of a sandwich filling. Try it in the *Roast Peppers with Walnut Vinaigrette and Sorrel* recipe (page 74)

MAKES 200 ml (7 fl oz)

50 g (2 oz) walnut pieces
2 tablespoons mixed chopped fresh herbs (such as parsley, thyme, rosemary, tarragon)
½ teaspoon Dijon mustard
2 tablespoons white wine vinegar

1 clove garlic, peeled and crushed
Salt and freshly ground black pepper
150 ml (5 fl oz) mixed walnut oil and olive oil

Pre-heat the oven to 190°C/375°F/gas 5 and toast the walnuts on a baking tray for 3–5 minutes. Using a blender or food processor, grind the walnuts finely.

Then add the herbs and blend thoroughly for a few seconds. Add the mustard, vinegar, garlic and seasoning. Blend again and gradually add the oils whilst the food processor or blender is still operating. Store in a clean jar and use within a week.

Avocado and Melon Salad with Pesto and Walnut Dressing

Walnut oil is mixed with pine kernels here to make an intensely flavoured pesto dressing.

Serve this refreshing summer salad on a large platter as part of a buffet meal. Alternatively arrange small portions on individual plates as a first course.

SERVES 4

For the dressing

50 g (2 oz) pine kernels
8 tablespoons walnut oil
2 tablespoons lemon juice
2–3 cloves garlic, peeled and crushed

4 teaspoons pesto
Salt and freshly ground black pepper

For the salad

2 avocados
2 Italian beef tomatoes
1 bunch watercress
1 small cantaloupe or charantais
*   melon*

Pre-heat the oven to 200°C/400°F/gas 6.

Toast the pine kernels for 3–4 minutes on a baking tray.

Mix the remaining dressing ingredients together and season to taste. Place in a blender and add the pine kernels and grind until smooth.

For the salad, peel the avocados and slice them. Slice the tomatoes thickly. Clean and prepare the watercress and arrange the avocado and tomato slices on a bed of it. Drizzle over about half of the dressing. Scoop the melon into balls or cut it into cubes. Toss in the remaining dressing until well coated. Arrange the melon on top of the sliced avocados and tomatoes. Serve chilled.

Sesame Oil

This oil divides into two categories, toasted and untoasted. The untoasted oil is pale with a pleasing delicate flavour. With the toasted variety the flavours intensify and so too does the colour ranging from russet gold to deep brown. When it is so dark I sometimes wonder if the seeds haven't been slightly scorched. It is worth shopping around for a flavour that suits you. Supermarkets often stock one brand of this oil. Try oriental shops and wholefood shops for more choice.

I do occasionally begin a cooking process with sesame oil, but only in a recipe where the whole cooking time is short. Its strength comes over better when added as a flavouring at the end of cooking. It has a natural affinity with ginger, chilli, lime and shoyu. Mix these ingredients to make robust dressings and marinades.

Asparagus with Hot Sesame and Lemon Dressing

Asparagus can take a strongly flavoured dressing such as this sesame oil mayonnaise. If you don't have chilli oil, use a few drops of tabasco, or a small quantity of very finely chopped fresh chilli.

1 egg
150 ml (5 fl oz) sunflower oil
  mixed with a little Chilli Oil
  (see page 80)
2 tablespoons toasted sesame oil
Juice of ½ lemon

1 clove garlic, peeled and crushed
1 tablespoon rice wine or mild
  vinegar
Salt and freshly ground black
  pepper
2 bunches asparagus

To make the dressing, beat the egg in a processor or blender. Pour on the sunflower oil gradually to make a thick mayonnaise consistency. Add the sesame oil, lemon juice and garlic and blend again. Then thin down the dressing with vinegar. Season to taste.

Prepare the asparagus by trimming off the woody stems. Place in a tall saucepan of boiling water with the stems in the water and the tips above so that they steam. Cook for 8–10 minutes. Drain well and serve warm with the dressing in a small separate dish.

Marinated Tofu with Sesame Salad

Hot sesame roasted tofu has a delicious flavour which permeates the dressing. I use untoasted sesame oil. You can use toasted but the flavour can be quite strong.

SERVES 4

1 pack firm tofu
2 tablespoons sesame oil

For the dressing

3 tablespoons shoyu
2 tablespoons fresh orange juice
2 teaspoons chopped fresh
  lemon grass

2 teaspoons dark brown sugar
2 tablespoons dry sherry

100 g (4 oz) mangetout
1 orange, peeled and
  segmented

2 sticks celery, chopped
3 spring onions, chopped
2 teaspoons sesame seeds

OVERLEAF
*Baked Italian Tomatoes with Basil
and Balsamic Vinegar (page 93)*

Pre-heat the oven to 200°C/400°F/gas 6.

Chop the tofu into bite-sized pieces and toss in the sesame oil. Put the tofu on a baking sheet and bake for 10 minutes.

Meanwhile make the dressing by mixing all the ingredients together. Toss the hot tofu in the dressing and leave to cool.

Blanch the mangetout in boiling water for 1 minute. Drain and cool. To assemble the dish, mix the orange segments and the salad vegetables together, add the tofu and as much of the dressing as you need to make the salad moist. Garnish with sesame seeds.

Sunflower Oil

Sunflower oil is a good all-round cooking oil has a pleasant, light flavour and is ideal in dressings where it allows other flavours to dominate.

If you want a stronger-tasting sunflower oil, look for unrefined or cold-pressed varieties that are on sale in specialist healthfood or wholefood shops. See page 75.

Roasted Cashew and Beansprout Salad with Salted Lime Dressing

Sweet, sharp and salty flavours characterize this salad. I would try to buy beansprouts from a specialist healthfood shop rather than a supermarket as not only do they have a more home-grown look but they also have more colour and flavour. Serve the salad with rice for a light main course.

SERVES 4

For the dressing

Juice and zest of 1 lime
½ teaspoon salt

1 teaspoon brown sugar
2 tablespoons sunflower oil

For the salad

225 g (8 oz) sugar snap peas or mangetout
225 g (8 oz) carrots, cut into matchsticks

225 g (8 oz) mung beansprouts
50 g (2 oz) cashew nuts
2 tablespoons chopped fresh coriander

Pre-heat the oven to 200°C/400°F/gas 6.

Mix the dressing ingredients together. Blanch the sugar snap peas in boiling water for 1 minute, then drain and cool. Mix together with the carrots and mung beansprouts. Pour over the dressing and mix well. Roast the cashew nuts on a baking tray for 3–4 minutes, then chop coarsely.

Garnish the salad with the coriander and cashews just before serving.

Balsamic Vinegar

The darling of present-day foodies! Nevertheless this is not an ingredient to be over-looked even if you detect a hint of snobbishness. Balsamic vinegar does have a complexity of flavour and the more you pay the more apparent that is. Why does it cost so much? Balsamic vinegar is made from the juice of sweet Trebbiano grapes. It is not allowed to ferment, thus it stays sweet. A vinegar mother (a technical term for a starter) and wine vinegar are added and the end result stored in a wooden barrel. At the end of the year the vinegar is moved to a new barrel of a different wood. It loses some volume but takes on the flavour of the wood in the same way wine does when aged in oak for example. A true balsamic vinegar should be aged for a minimum of ten years, hence the staggering cost. A reasonable balsamic vinegar costs around £10.00. Anything substantially cheaper is made up with a fair amount of wine vinegar. Even so, it can be worth a try and you can always move up in price accordingly the next time you buy it.

Balsamic vinegar should be used sparingly as a condiment, sprinkled over fresh vegetables, added to salads. Strawberries with balsamic vinegar are fast becoming a classic dish.

Baked Italian Tomatoes with Basil and Balsamic Vinegar

These tomatoes make a bold splash of colour on the table. Serve them as part of a salad meal with *Melting Cheese Parcels* (page 101), *Marinated Feta with Sun-dried Tomatoes* (page 78), with a green salad, or as a side vegetable to accompany *Tortilla with Coriander and Parsley* (page 16) or *Warm Spinach and Roquefort Quiche* (page 117).

SERVES 4

4 large Italian beef tomatoes
4 tablespoons olive oil or Basil
   Oil (see page 81)
2 tablespoons balsamic vinegar
2 teaspoons chopped fresh basil

Salt and freshly ground black
   pepper
8 basil leaves
12 black olives, pitted

Pre-heat the oven to 190°C/375°F/gas 5.

Cut each tomato in half and arrange in a large shallow baking dish. Mix the oil, vinegar and chopped basil together, then season to taste. Dip each basil leaf in the dressing and place on the tomatoes. Pour the remaining dressing over the tomato halves.

Bake for 15 minutes or until the tomatoes are just tender. Baste occasionally. When cooked, spoon any juices over the tomatoes and leave to cool. Serve at room temperature, garnished with the olives.

Grilled Courgettes with Balsamic Vinegar

Grilled courgettes taste sweeter than raw ones. Only cook them until they are just coloured and still crisp.

SERVES 4

50 g (2 oz) walnut halves
225 g (8 oz) courgettes
3–4 whole sun-dried tomatoes
   (in oil), very finely diced
100 g (4 oz) tinned chick peas,
   drained
3 tablespoons oil from the sun-
   dried tomatoes or olive oil

1 tablespoon balsamic vinegar
2–3 teaspoons fresh marjoram
   or oregano
1 tablespoon chopped fresh
   parsley
Salt and freshly ground black
   pepper

Lightly toast the walnuts under the grill or in a hot oven for 3–4 minutes.

Slice the courgettes thinly on the diagonal. Grill under a very high heat until lightly toasted. Mix in a bowl with the sun-dried tomatoes, chick peas and walnuts.

Mix the oil and balsamic vinegar and herbs. Toss into the salad ingredients. Season to taste. Leave to cool.

FRESH CHEESES CREAMS AND YOGHURT

I remember as a child queueing with my mother at the dairy counter in the local supermarket. Served by a lady in a white coat, hair covered by an unfaltering net, we had a choice of about five cheeses, pats of butter, eggs and that was it. Now supermarkets seem to have an endless procession of dairy products. I should hastily say that it is not just at supermarkets where you'll find a good selection of interesting dairy products. Thank goodness for the specialist cheese shop, or well-informed delicatessen as well as the upsurge in small dairies producing splendid cheeses.

I love being confronted by something new, which of course I have to try! Some items are disappointing, but in amongst the profusion there are always some gems. Moreish melting soft cheese, tangy leaf-wrapped goat's cheese, and a host of imported cheeses that all have their own distinctive character.

Where to begin? In this chapter I'll look at the best of the fresh soft cheeses, near creams and creams that are so useful in cooking today. There has been a proliferation of soft fresh cheeses and creams recently. They are characterized by their mild flavour, and come in various shades of white. Some have the consistency of double cream, some just hold their shape, some will spread, others will slice. Their richness depends on their fat content. A few have been around a long time and I mean this in terms of supermarket availability rather than historically – for example, cottage cheese or cream cheese. But plenty of new names are now on the shelves such as crème fraîche, fromage frais and mascarpone, to name but a few. In this chapter, I've described some of my favourites followed by an appropriate recipe.

Buying and Storing
All fresh cheese, creams and so on must be stored in the fridge. Sell-by dates are often quite lengthy. Do use the cheese up in that time. If you get any of these sorts of products from a farm or delicatessen, they may need to be eaten within just a few days.

Crème Fraîche

Crème Fraîche is a French version of soured cream. Like soured cream it has a pleasant, delicate tang but its high fat content makes it taste richer. Crème fraîche works well in both sweet and savoury dishes. At its simplest it is delicious spooned over fruit, used as a casserole topping or served with a baked potato. It is equally good when cooked. Its high fat content means that it can be boiled without separating which makes it more versatile and foolproof than plain cream. Use crème fraîche to enrich soups and sauces.

Aubergine Mousse with Crème Fraîche

In this mousse, the crème fraîche lightens and enriches the mixture. Its mild sour flavour works well with the aromatic cumin seeds.

SERVES 4

50 g (2 oz) shelled walnuts
1 teaspoon cumin seeds
1 large aubergine
1 clove garlic, peeled and crushed

100 g (4 oz) crème fraîche
Salt and freshly ground black
*   pepper*

Pre-heat the oven to 200°C/400°F/gas 6.

Toast the walnuts for 4–5 minutes on a baking tray and also toast the cumin seeds lightly for 2–3 minutes. Then grind both finely.

Bake the aubergine at the same oven temperature for 30–40 minutes or until fairly soft. Scrape out the flesh and leave to cool. Put into a food processor or blender. Add the garlic, toasted nuts, seeds and crème fraîche and blend until smooth. Season to taste. Leave to stand before serving for the flavours to blend. Serve at room temperature.

Buckwheat Pancakes with Lentils and Crème Fraîche

Crème fraîche adds a certain luxury to lentils. This soft filling, well-flavoured with leeks and thyme, is good with the mild sour taste of buckwheat. Serve these pancakes with a sauce such as the *Tomato and Fresh Herb Sauce* on page 124.

SERVES 4

For the pancakes

300 ml (10 fl oz) milk
1 egg
1 teaspoon oil
50 g (2 oz) buckwheat flour

50 g (2 oz) wholemeal flour
A pinch of salt
A little oil for frying

For the filling

175 g (6 oz) red lentils
300 ml (10 fl oz) boiling water
50 g (2 oz) butter
350 g (12 oz) leeks, trimmed and chopped
1 teaspoon chopped fresh thyme

175 ml (6 fl oz) crème fraîche
25 g (1 oz) ground almonds
Salt and freshly ground black pepper
2–3 teaspoons sesame seeds
Butter for brushing (optional)

Using a food processor or blender, mix the milk, egg and oil together for 30 seconds. Then add the flours and salt and blend again until smooth. Leave the batter to rest for 20 minutes.

Using a small, preferably non-stick frying-pan, heat a little oil and when the pan is smoking, add 2 tablespoons batter and fry the pancake for 2–3 minutes on either side. Make 8 pancakes in the same way. Once cooked pile them up on a plate and keep warm.

Meanwhile, cook the lentils in the boiling water for 25–30 minutes or until the water is absorbed and the lentils have become a thick purée. In a separate pan melt the butter, add the leeks and cook until tender. Stir in the thyme. Off the heat, mix in the lentils, crème fraîche and almonds. Season to taste.

Fill each pancake using 3 tablespoons of the stuffing mixture. Roll up and place in an ovenproof dish. Sprinkle with sesame seeds and heat through in a microwave. Alternatively, brush with melted butter then sprinkle with sesame seeds, cover with foil and heat in the oven before serving.

Fresh Goat's Cheese and Soft Goat's Cheese

Fresh goat's cheese is very like fromage frais but made with goat's milk instead of cow's. It doesn't have the smooth texture of fromage frais, but will nevertheless blend well with other soft cheeses and creams.

Goat's milk gives even the freshest of cheeses a distinctive tang. The flavour should develop with age. The youngest cheeses are snow-white and sometimes sold wrapped round with leaves which can give the cheese a hint of citrus.

I've included recipes using soft goat's cheese in this chapter. Strictly speaking the cheeses are not fresh and have begun the ripening process. The riper goat's cheese is, the stronger it tastes but its texture can remain quite soft. You can choose either a strong or relatively mild cheese for both recipes. (There are more notes on goat's cheese on page 107.)

Individual Celeriac and Goat's Cheese Timbales

A very fresh goat's cheese is just a little too mild for this recipe. You need a stronger tang to compliment the nutty flavour of the celeriac but don't go for a well-ripened variety as it won't blend easily into the mixture. Buy quite a young cheese that has a good flavour but still a soft texture.

Serve these timbales with a sauce such as the *Roasted Garlic Sauce* on page 235.

SERVES 4

1 tablespoon sunflower oil
1 onion, finely chopped
1 clove garlic, peeled and crushed
350 g (12 oz) celeriac, peeled and grated
2 tablespoons white wine

100 g (4 oz) soft goat's cheese
1 tablespoon chopped fresh parsley
2 eggs, beaten
Salt and freshly ground black pepper

PREVIOUS PAGES
Left: *Melting Cheese Parcels* (page 101)
Right: *Tomato and Fennel Soup with Tarragon and Mascarpone* (page 103)

Heat the oil and cook the onion and garlic gently, without colouring, for 4–5 minutes. Add the grated celeriac and mix in well. Then add the white wine and cook until the celeriac is just soft. Add a little water if necessary. Remove the pan from the heat.

Mash the cheese with a fork, then mix into the celeriac with the parsley and beaten eggs. Season well.

Pre-heat the oven to 180°C/350°F/gas 4.

Spoon the mixture into 4 well-greased individual pudding basins. (Ramekins will do though the finished shape is not so good.) Set the basins in a bain-marie and bake for 30 minutes or until the timbales have just set. Turn out and serve hot.

Melting Cheese Parcels

It is the melting texture of the cheese which make these tiny filo parcels so moreish. Choose a soft goat's cheese, either mild or strong in flavour. The triangles can be made in different sizes, but I have found less cheese leaks out in smaller ones. I occasionally serve these as a starter but they really make splendid party fare. If you are making a selection for a buffet or picnic, try adding some of the flavourings I've suggested.

MAKES 12–16 parcels

50 g (2 oz) butter
50 ml (2 fl oz) olive oil
12–16 sheets filo pastry
  (see page 47)

175–225 g (6–8 oz) soft goat's
  cheese

Suggested flavourings (optional)

Crushed garlic
Chopped fresh herbs (such as
  chives, basil, thyme, parsley)

Chopped roasted pepper
Crushed peppercorns

Melt the butter with the olive oil. Make sure the filo pastry is thoroughly defrosted. Take 1 sheet at a time, brush liberally with the melted butter and olive oil. Fold the pastry in half to make a long strip. Place a small wedge of goat's cheese at one end [about 15 g (½ oz)]. If you wish to add any flavourings, put a teaspoon or so on top of the cheese. Roll the pastry up around the wedge to make a triangle shape. Brush well again with the melted butter mixture. Repeat with the remaining filo pastry sheets and cheese.

Bake the parcels on a greased baking sheet for 20 minutes or until the pastry is crisp and golden. Serve warm or at room temperature.

Fromage Frais

Flavoured fromage frais is very popular with my children. The tiny pots appeal, as well as the brightly coloured packaging. I vet the contents list for gelatine, E numbers and vague terms such as 'flavourings'. Even the purest are heavily sweetened. I have to confess that, whilst my two are allowed to gobble them up as an occasional treat, to me they have little flavour and a cloying texture. How different from the unadulterated fromage frais with its clean tang.

Fromage frais is a soft unripened cheese made from cow's milk. The curd is beaten until very smooth. Fromage frais spoons out rather than pours as it has the texture of strained yoghurt. The fat content of fromage frais is variable. There are diet or low-fat fromage frais as well as richer varieties to which cream has been added.

Fromage frais is great on its own, or lightly sweetened and mixed with fresh or dried fruits it makes a creamy dessert. You can also use it as a base for savoury dips and salad dressing. Fromage frais with a higher fat content is suitable for cooking as it shouldn't separate. Even so take care when adding it to hot sauces.

On the whole I switch to crème fraîche if I want a tangy cooking soft cheese. I prefer to make simple recipes with fromage frais so that its clean taste comes through.

Roasted Hazelnut and Fromage Frais Dip

This fresh-tasting dip is best for raw vegetables. Choose a colourful
selection to include carrot, celery sticks, peppers and cucumber.

MAKES 300 g (11 OZ)

50 g (2 oz) shelled hazelnuts
1 teaspoon cider vinegar
2 tablespoons hazelnut oil
3–4 tablespoons olive oil
175 g (6 oz) fromage frais

2 tablespoons snipped fresh
chives
Salt and freshly ground black
pepper

Pre-heat the oven to 200°C/400°F/gas 6 and roast the hazelnuts on a baking tray for 5 minutes. Leave to cool, then rub off the skins. Put the nuts in a nut mill or blender and grind until fairly smooth. Add the cider vinegar and grind again, then add the oils, blending continuously to make a thicker cream. Mix or blend in the fromage frais. Stir in the chives and season to taste.

Leave to stand for an hour before serving.

Mascarpone

Mascarpone is a very rich cream cheese, the consistency of clotted cream. It is made from fresh cream which is whipped to give it a very smooth texture. In Italy, from where mascarpone originates, it is principally used as a dessert cheese. It can replace or be mixed with custard or yoghurt, or spiked with liqueur and served with fruit.

It works equally well in savoury dishes. Its high fat content means it is very unlikely to separate. Added to soups and sauces it gives them a velvet richness. It can also be used in dips, quiche and pancake fillings. (See *Mushroom Parfait with Mascarpone and White Wine* on page 33.)

Tomato and Fennel Soup with Tarragon and Mascarpone

Fresh tomatoes have a good flavour but mean that the finished soup is paler than soup made with tinned tomatoes.

In this soup mascarpone is added towards the end of cooking to give body to the soup as well as a creamy taste.

SERVES 4

2 tablespoons olive oil
1 onion, chopped
1 clove garlic, peeled and crushed
1 head fennel (weighing about 225 g/8 oz), trimmed and chopped
450 g (1 lb) fresh tomatoes, skinned and chopped
8 sun-dried tomatoes (in oil)
1 tablespoon chopped fresh chives
1 tablespoon chopped fresh oregano
1 tablespoon chopped fresh parsley
1 tablespoon chopped fresh tarragon
1 tablespoon tomato purée
300 ml (10 fl oz) vegetable stock
100 g (4 oz) mascarpone cheese
Salt and freshly ground black pepper

Heat the oil and gently fry the onion and garlic until soft. Next add the fennel and cook for about 10 minutes over a gentle heat. Add the skinned tomatoes, sun-dried tomatoes, herbs, tomato purée and stock. Bring the mixture to the boil and simmer for 25–30 minutes. Leave to cool, then add the mascarpone and blend or sieve until smooth. Season well and re-heat before serving.

Ricotta

Compared to all the other very soft cheeses in this chapter, ricotta with its slightly crumbly curd-like texture seems the most cheese-like of them all. It's odd to realize that it is not really a cheese at all as it is traditionally made from whey and not curds.

If you are lucky enough to have a good Italian shop near you, it is worth buying fresh ricotta which is much better than the pre-packaged cheese sold in plastic tubs.

Ricotta should be snow-white with a bland taste. It can be eaten solo, but I prefer to mix it in with other ingredients. With something like spinach, ricotta blends well, keeps the texture light and yet adds a clean flavour. It works very well with many other vegetables and is good for lasagne sauces or pastry fillings. Partner ricotta with other cheeses such as mascarpone for a richer mix.

Stuffed Tomatoes with Ricotta and Basil

These make a light creamy addition to a main meal when served with buttered baby spinach and bread or pasta in a simple sauce. The tomatoes should be as ripe as possible.

SERVES 4

4 Italian beef tomatoes
Salt and freshly ground black pepper
2 tablespoons olive oil
1 onion, finely chopped
1 clove garlic, peeled and crushed
150 g (5 oz) ricotta
2 tablespoons chopped fresh basil
25 g (1 oz) fresh Parmesan, grated
25 g (1 oz) fresh breadcrumbs

Slice a lid off the top of each tomato and cut out the core and seeds but do not discard. Season the insides well then turn upside-down and leave to drain for 15 minutes. Meanwhile, heat the oil and fry the onion and garlic until very soft but not coloured.

Pre-heat the oven to 190°C/375°F/gas 5.

Chop the tomato flesh and then strain the seeds, adding this juice along with the tomato flesh to the onions and reduce the mixture to a thick pulp. Off the heat stir in the ricotta and basil and half the Parmesan. Season to taste. Divide this mixture between the four tomatoes. Sprinkle over the breadcrumbs and then the remaining Parmesan.

Place in an oiled, ovenproof dish and bake for 25 minutes. Serve hot.

Yoghurt

I have two very clear memories of yoghurt. The first from a cycling holiday in France when I was about ten. We discovered these pots of almost solid white stuff, which was sharp, sour and creamy all at the same time. Much later, I remember the arrival of Greek yoghurt. I thought it was ambrosia, velvet smooth, rich, but with a hint of sharpness.

Today's yoghurts still range through this spectrum. They can be made from cow's, sheep's or goat's milk. Each has a slightly different flavour. If you like very sharp natural yoghurt, I think it is worth trying some of the organic varieties now sold. For a delicate yet creamy yoghurt, try the bio yoghurts where bacteria used to culture the milk give it the mildest flavour. Greek yoghurt is strained to get rid of excess whey. The end result is thicker, the flavour more concentrated. Which yoghurt to use for dips, dressings and desserts is a matter of personal taste. Cooking with yoghurt demands care as it can curdle extremely easily. I find a strained yoghurt less fragile, but add it to the hot mixture gradually as in the following recipe.

Cauliflower and Broad Beans with Greek Yoghurt

Cauliflower and broad beans make a good pair, contrasting in both texture and colour, yet their flavours work well together. Fresh broad beans are marvellous but frozen work reasonably well.

SERVES 4

175 g (6 oz) shelled broad beans
3 tablespoons sunflower oil
1 onion, finely chopped
2 cloves garlic, peeled and
    crushed
½ teaspoon turmeric
2 teaspoons garam masala
2 tablespoons sesame seeds

350 g (12 oz) cauliflower
    divided into small florets
300 ml (10 fl oz) Greek-style
    natural yoghurt
2 tablespoons fresh lemon juice
Salt and freshly ground black
    pepper

Cook the beans for 10 minutes. Drain and set aside. Heat the oil and gently fry the onion until quite soft. Add the garlic, then the spices and sesame seeds and fry for 2–3 minutes. Next add the cauliflower florets and cooked broad beans and coat well with the spice mixture. Put on the lid and cook for 5 minutes. Add the yoghurt 1 tablespoon at a time so it doesn't curdle, then add lemon juice to taste. Season and serve immediately.

OTHER CHEESES

I am lucky enough to live within a short walk of a wonderful shop which stocks over a hundred different French and English cheeses. Nipping in there for a sliver of sharp Lancashire, or a goat's cheese so shrunken and mouldy you'd think it was going to leave the shop of its own accord, has taught me a new appreciation of fine cheese.

The following notes are specifically to help you buy cheese for eating rather than for cooking. Later on in this chapter you'll find details of a few of my favourite cheeses with accompanying recipes.

Mould-ripened Cheeses

This family includes cheeses such as Brie and Camembert. The ripeness of these cheeses is critical to their flavour and texture. Ripening makes the flavour of the cheese less acidic. The ripening process also makes the cheese soft, giving it that characteristic runnyness when at room temperature. If the cheese is very firm, it is not ready to be eaten. Apart from feeling a cheese to see if it is ripe, you may also see patches of pink or orange mould on the surface. When buying a piece you should try to get advice on these cheeses from someone who can tell you when the cheese is at its best. Once cut, a piece will not mature in the same way as a whole cheese. It's no good thinking on Thursday that a slightly under-ripe piece will be perfect for Sunday lunch. Better in that case to buy a whole small cheese. Brie is always made as a large cheese, Camembert can be small. Look out for Bonchester, quite small and expensive, but worth it.

Keep mould-ripened cheeses in the fridge, but remember they must be at room temperature when you are ready to eat. Allow 2–3 hours for this.

Goat's Cheese

Mould-ripened cheeses go from hard to soft as they ripen but with goat's cheese it is the reverse. The harder the cheese the stronger will be the flavour. Chèvre frais (fresh goat's cheese) has just the hint of a goaty tang whereas the riper cheeses have a marvellous up-your-nose pungency.

Goat's cheeses often develop quite spectacular moulds. Don't worry, these are edible. Whilst the moulds may vigorously cover the surface, once cut, it is often almost entirely superficial, leaving a distinctive bone-white interior.

Blue Cheese

Roquefort is Roquefort and there is nothing quite like it. Probably the mildest in this range is dolcelatte. In between there are a wealth of flavours – sweet, sharp, creamy, toffee. Flavour has nothing to do with the amount of blue.

English Stilton should be moist and creamy and certainly not gouged out in the middle. A less well-known English blue is the Devon Blue. Look out too for Cashel Blue, quite runny when in peak condition.

Traditional British Cheese

Beware the word Farmhouse! It has rustic undertones but is often applied to cheese which hasn't been within fifty miles of a farm. A proper cheese is made in a truckle, a stone-coloured cylindrical block. Cheese cut from these often has a rind. Cheese in good condition should not look dry, nor should it sweat. Any cracks, or a darker colour towards the outside are a sign it is past its best.

It is virtually impossible to recommend a traditional British cheese which is also available countrywide. Look out for Keen's Cheddar, Devon Oke, and Duckett's Caerphilly. There are also some excellent Irish cheeses.

Storing Cheese

Apart from the mould-ripened family (Brie etc.), if kept well cheeses will remain in good condition for quite some time. Ripened cheese should be kept in the fridge. The best wrapping is waxed paper, next best greaseproof. Cling film simply doesn't let the cheese breathe. If you have the space, keep the cheese, cut surfaces covered, in a tub, then cover that with a damp cloth.

For a cheeseboard, I would advise getting no more than three decent-sized pieces of really good cheese. Lots of small pieces are hard to keep in good condition, and if the tastes are really memorable you don't want too many of them. Sometimes I serve just one small whole cheese.

Cashel Blue

Cashel Blue is a semi-soft blue-veined cow's milk cheese made in Tipperary, Ireland. When young it has a dry almost crumbly texture. As the cheese matures it becomes softer with a tendency to runnyness. It has a mild flavour but with a very pleasing tang that is quite elusive. This cheese, whilst it is the second biggest-selling Irish farmhouse cheese, is hard to get in this country. Look for it in a specialist cheese shop or delicatessen.

New Potato Salad with Blue Cheese Dressing

Cashel Blue makes a marvellous creamy dressing for new potatoes that is flavourful but not too strong. The crisp texture of apple and celery contrast well with the rich dressing.

SERVES 4

450 g (1 lb) new potatoes
100 g (4 oz) Cashel Blue cheese
6 tablespoons mayonnaise
2 tablespoons snipped fresh
    chives

1 red eating apple, cored and
    diced
2 sticks of celery, diced
Salt and freshly ground black
    pepper

Scrub the potatoes and boil until tender in lightly salted water. Leave to cool.

Meanwhile make the dressing. Mash the cheese with the mayonnaise. Mix in the chives. Add the other ingredients, then add the potatoes when still slightly warm and season to taste. Serve at room temperature.

Pear Soup with Cashel Blue and Paprika Croûtons

This soup has a wonderful fresh tang with its mixture of pears and Cashel Blue. You can use other blue cheese but go for the sharper tastes rather than anything too salty. This soup is very quick to prepare. I like to garnish it with these croûtons lightly spiced with paprika. As with many fruit soups, it is best served in small portions.

SERVES 4

2 tablespoons sunflower oil
1 onion, chopped
2 pears, peeled, cored and
    chopped
300 ml (10 fl oz) vegetable stock

½ teaspoon paprika
Juice of ½ lemon
150 g (5 oz) Cashel Blue cheese
Salt and freshly ground black
    pepper

For the croûtons

2 slices wholemeal bread
3 tablespoons olive oil
½ teaspoon paprika

Heat the oil and gently fry the onion until soft. Add the pears and stock and bring to the boil. Cook for 5–10 minutes or until the pears are very soft. Leave to cool, then purée in a food processor with the paprika, lemon juice and cheese until smooth. Sieve for a very smooth texture. Season to taste.

For the croûtons pre-heat the oven to 200°C/400°F/gas 6. Cut the bread into cubes. Season the oil and mix in the paprika. Toss in the cubes, place on baking parchment and bake in a hot oven until crisp.

Gently heat the soup through, then serve garnished with croûtons.

Cheddar

I had to include a separate mention of Cheddar cheese as it is such a useful ingredient. For cooking I'm content to use a prepacked block from a supermarket, but it is worth seeking out handmade Cheddar cheese which has a wonderful flavour.

Quesadillas with Roasted Tomatoes

Quesadillas are cheese-filled tortillas. You can buy unfilled tortillas from large supermarkets. This quick snack makes a warming change from a sandwich. I also make quesadillas as an accompaniment to a spicy stew or gumbo (see *Sweet Potato Gumbo* on page 65). They are good served with *Salsa Verde* (page 24), or *Guacamole* (see page 197) and soured cream.

SERVES 4

2–3 tomatoes
Salt and freshly ground black
pepper
4–6 tortillas

75 g (3 oz) grated Cheddar
1 tablespoon chopped fresh
coriander

Pre-heat the oven to 200°C/400°F/gas 6.

Cut the tomatoes in half and roast on a baking tray for 5 minutes or until just soft. Remove the skins and season the flesh.

To make the quesadillas, heat a small heavy-based frying-pan. Dry-fry each tortilla so that it starts to brown on the underneath. Cover half the tortilla with a portion of grated Cheddar, the flesh of half a tomato and a little coriander. Season to taste, fold the other half over and heat through. Turn over and cook until the cheese has melted. Quickly cut in wedges and serve hot.

Feta

Feta cheese is traditionally made from ewe's milk. It should be very white, moist and crumbly. It has a characteristic salty, almost sour, flavour. This is because when feta is made the curds are salted and then covered with a mixture of whey and brine. The cheese is then left for a few days to pickle.

Feta is commonly served cubed in salads with olives, tomatoes and other traditional Greek fare. It's delicious when marinated (see *Marinated Feta with Sun-dried Tomatoes* on page 78). I have only recently found how well it works cooked. It doesn't melt or brown in the way other cheeses do but it has a creamy texture and its distinctive taste comes through. Its strong taste marries well with olives and tomatoes when used as a topping for pizzas too (see *Pizza Dough with Olive Oil* on page 193).

Tian of Artichoke, Feta
and Bulgar Wheat

This is an attractive supper dish of bulgar wheat and vegetables baked in a Feta sauce. It is easy to prepare and needs only a light salad or two to make a good meal.

SERVES 4

1 onion, chopped
2 cloves garlic, peeled and
    crushed
100 g (4 oz) bulgar wheat
250 ml (8 fl oz) water
½ teaspoon salt
12–15 olives
4 artichoke hearts in oil,
    quartered

175 g (6 oz) feta cheese
4 eggs
2 tablespoons chopped fresh
    basil
2 tablespoons chopped fresh
    parsley
2 teaspoons pesto
Salt and freshly ground black
    pepper

Heat the oil and gently fry the onion and garlic. Stir in the bulgar wheat and cook for 2–3 minutes. Pour over the water and add the salt. Bring to the boil, then simmer for 5 minutes until all the water is absorbed and the bulgar wheat is soft.

Pre-heat the oven to 190°C/375°F/gas 5.

Spoon the bulgar into an oiled shallow ovenproof dish. Arrange the olives and artichokes over the top.

Purée the Feta cheese with the eggs, herbs and pesto to make a smooth sauce. Season to taste. Pour this over the bulgar wheat. Bake for 30 minutes. Serve hot.

Haloumi

Haloumi is a semi-hard Cypriot cheese made from ewe's milk. It is usually sold in rectangular blocks which can be sliced or cubed. Although it is not a cheese that works well with prolonged cooking as it hardens rather than melts, it does work well if slightly roasted or grilled. This seems to bring out its delicate minty flavour. Try also the *Haloumi Cheese Brochettes with Hot Pineapple* on page 215.

Baked Haloumi with Walnut Croûtons

The cheese is just baked for a few minutes giving it a slightly firmer texture. Serve it with robust walnut croûtons made from wholemeal bread or lighter croûtons made of white bread. You can also ring the changes by using a different oil such as hazelnut oil, untoasted sesame oil or a good-quality olive oil.

To make an interesting summer spread you can serve this salad with extra bread, *Baked Italian Tomatoes with Basil and Balsamic Vinegar* (page 93) and *Marinated Mushrooms* (see page 84).

SERVES 4

175 g (6 oz) haloumi cheese
2 thick slices wholemeal bread
5 tablespoons walnut oil
Salt and freshly ground black pepper

25 g (1 oz) walnut halves
Small cos lettuce leaves
24 black olives, pitted
16 cherry tomatoes, halved
6–8 sprigs of fresh mint

Pre-heat the oven to 200°C/400°F/gas 6.

Slice or cube the haloumi. Bake on a baking tray lined with baking parchment for 5 minutes or until just beginning to brown.

Cut the bread into small cubes. Put 3 tablespoons of walnut oil and seasoning in a small bowl and toss in the bread cubes. Bake these on parchment in the oven for 5 minutes or until quite crisp. Leave to cool.

Toast the walnut halves in the oven for 3–4 minutes and leave to cool.

To assemble the salad, line a plate or bowl with cos lettuce leaves, arrange the cubes of haloumi, olives and tomatoes on top. Then sprinkle over the remaining walnut oil. Top with the toasted walnut halves, croûtons and sprigs of mint.

Mozzarella

Mozzarella is a distinguished Italian curd cheese which was once only made from buffalo milk. It has a spongy texture, just firm enough to slice and melts beautifully, creating long tasty strings. It is a wonderful topping for pizza and gratin dishes.

For salads too you should buy really fresh mozzarella. It is worth splashing out on the best if you can find it. A classic recipe is to partner it with thickly sliced Italian tomatoes. Fresh mozzarella should be stored in the refrigerator covered in fresh water.

You may find mozzarella produced by countries other than Italy. Some of these don't have quite such good melting qualities. A yellow hard grated mozzarella is also sold. This should only be used for cooking. Frankly it is one of the few new ingredients that I have never tried because I so like the real McCoy.

Aubergine and Tomato Galette

Make this simple dish with the best ingredients as the individual flavours do stand out. Use a good-quality olive oil, firm aubergines, plump tomatoes and fresh herbs. Finish with mozzarella and you have a superb supper dish.

SERVES 4

900 g (2 lb) aubergines (about 3
 medium-sized ones)
5 tablespoons olive oil
1 onion, finely chopped
2 cloves garlic, peeled and
 crushed
450 g (1 lb) fresh plum tomatoes,
 peeled and chopped
2–3 tablespoons finely chopped
 sun-dried tomatoes (in oil)

2 teaspoons chopped fresh
 oregano
1 teaspoon chopped fresh
 rosemary
1 teaspoon chopped fresh thyme
Salt and freshly ground black
 pepper
100 g (4 oz) mozzarella, sliced
2–3 tablespoons freshly grated
 Parmesan

Pre-heat the oven to 190°C/375°F/gas 5.

Slice the aubergines into thick slices and brush with 2–3 tablespoons olive oil. Put on an oiled tray and bake for 30 minutes. The slices should be soft and slightly browned.

Using 2 tablespoons olive oil, gently fry the onion and garlic until soft. Add the chopped plum tomatoes and sun-dried tomatoes, then cook for 10 minutes. Mix in the fresh herbs. Season to taste. Cover the base of a large shallow ovenproof dish with most of the onion and tomato mixture, then with all the aubergine slices. Use the remaining tomato mixture. Cover with slices of mozzarella, then sprinkle over the Parmesan. Bake for 35–40 minutes. Serve hot.

Parmesan

Parmesan belongs to a group of Italian cheeses known as 'grana' (i.e. hard and grainy). Under strict rules of production it has to be matured for at least eighteen months. The cheese itself is straw-coloured with an intense aromatic flavour.

Parmesan is most frequently used as a finishing touch for pasta, gratin dishes and pizzas. Its close texture means it can be grated very finely. But beware! Once grated, the aroma soon disappears. Try comparing some Parmesan sold dried and ready grated to some freshly grated. They bear little resemblance.

It is best to buy whole pieces of Parmesan. Wrap it in foil and it will keep for several weeks in the refrigerator.

Parmesan shavings are fashionable but they are also fun and certainly liven up salads and sandwich mixtures. Make the shavings using a Scandinavian cheese slicer.

OVERLEAF
Left: *Warm Spinach and Roquefort Quiche* (page 117)
Right: *Baked Haloumi with Walnut Croûtons* (page 111)

Parmesan and Potato Cakes

This recipe idea is loosely based on the potato gnocchi that features in cuisine from Northern Italy. My version is baked, making the cakes a little more solid perhaps, but certainly more foolproof. Serve these cakes with a little extra Parmesan and a tomato sauce or spoonful of pesto.

SERVES 4

550 g (1¼ lb) potatoes
1 onion, finely diced
4 sticks celery, diced
2 cloves garlic, peeled and crushed
25 g (1 oz) butter
2 eggs, beaten

75 g (3 oz) fresh Parmesan, grated
150 ml (5 fl oz) double cream
2 tablespoon chopped fresh parsley
Salt and freshly ground black pepper

Peel and boil the potatoes, then mash until smooth.

Fry the onion, celery and garlic in the butter until soft. Mix the onion mixture with the beaten eggs, grated Parmesan, cream, parsley and mashed potatoes. Season well.

Pre-heat the oven to 200°C/400°F/gas 6.

Butter and base line 8 large ramekins or individual dishes. Divide the mixture between the ramekins. Bake for 20 minutes. Turn out and serve hot.

Roquefort

You know when you are eating Roquefort. This ivory-coloured cheese with its blue-green veining has a strong salty flavour. It melts in the mouth but has a full aftertaste. You also know you've bought a piece of Roquefort if your purse feels considerably lighter. Roquefort is the platinum of the cheese world. It is very expensive, but for certain dishes worth it.

Where you need a bold flavour, use it. This is why I think Roquefort works particularly well in the quiche recipe below.

Warm Spinach and Roquefort Quiche

It is important in this recipe to cook the spinach until it is really dry. This will mean that you reduce its bulk considerably, retaining the flavour, but you won't end up with a watery filling.

SERVES 4–6

For the pastry

*75 g (3 oz) butter or solid
    vegetable fat
175 g (6 oz) plain white flour or
    wholemeal flour
1 egg yolk beaten
2–3 tablespoons cold water*

For the filling

25 g (1 oz) butter
2 shallots, chopped
1 clove garlic, peeled and crushed
*450 g (1 lb) spinach, washed and
    chopped*

3 eggs
100 g (4 oz) Roquefort
150 ml (5 fl oz) crème fraîche
*Salt and freshly ground black
    pepper*

For the pastry, rub the fat into the flour. Add the egg yolk and enough water to make a soft dough. Add more water if necessary, especially if you are using wholemeal flour. Cover with cling film and leave to rest in the fridge for 30 minutes. Roll out thinly to fill a 25 cm (10 in) flan dish.

Melt the butter and gently fry the shallots and garlic. Add the spinach and cook over a high heat until the spinach reduces and all the liquid has evaporated. Drain once or twice during cooking if necessary. Chop finely. Mix the eggs, cheese and crème fraîche until smooth. Add the cooked spinach. Season to taste.

Pre-heat the oven to 200°C/400°F/gas 6.

Roll out the pastry to fill a 20–23 cm (8–9 inch) flan case and pour over the spinach mixture. Bake for 35–40 minutes. Serve warm.

Stilton

Stilton is the best known and most widely available of English blue cheeses. It is made under a strict trademark and can only legally be produced in the three shires of Leicester, Nottingham and Derby.

A good Stilton should be smooth and creamy, certainly not dry or crumbly. This can be a sign that it isn't mature or simply hasn't been kept properly. It is not easy to know if Stilton is at its best just by looking. Try to buy Stilton from someone who will tell you when it is ready or, better still, let you have a taste first.

Stilton Choux with Stilton and Watercress Cream

Choux pastry can take a strong ingredient such as Stilton, both in the dough and in the filling. These choux make an attractive light meal when served with a couple of salads or can be part of a buffet spread.

SERVES 4

For the choux pastry

150 ml (5 fl oz) water	*2 eggs*
50 g (2 oz) butter	*50 g (2 oz) Stilton*
50 g (2 oz) plain flour	*¼ teaspoon prepared mustard*

For the filling

100 g (4 oz) Stilton	*4 tablespoons chopped fresh*
6 tablespoons double	*watercress*
cream	*Freshly ground black pepper*

Pre-heat the oven to 200°C/400°F/gas 6.

Put the water and butter in a saucepan and bring to the boil. When boiling and the butter melted, remove the pan from the heat and shoot in all the flour. Beat until very glossy. Beat in the eggs one at a time. Next add the cheese and mustard and beat again.

Divide the mixture into 12 spoonfuls on baking parchment. Bake for 20 minutes, then reduce the temperature to 190°C/375°F/gas 5 and bake for a further 5–10 minutes. It is best if the pastry is quite crisp or it can collapse. When the buns are cooked remove from the oven and split open, then leave to cool.

To make the filling, grate or mash the Stilton, then mix it with the other ingredients and season with pepper. Fill each bun with a little of the Stilton cream.

PASTA AND POLENTA

I don't think it is an overstatement to say we have a passion for pasta. It is a wonderful food and these days comes in a wide variety of shapes and seemingly an endless number of colours from yellow to black.

Dried wholemeal pasta is part of my kitchen stock. My children love it and I use it particularly for substantial pasta bakes and layered dishes. When making lighter recipes, such as those with a simple sauce, my preference is for fresh pasta, plain or flavoured. It is quick to cook and when cooked correctly has a light, almost melting, quality.

In this chapter I've started with several sauce recipes that are ideal with fresh pasta, (though of course use wholemeal dried versions if you wish), a filling for ravioli and finally two lasagne recipes.

Further on in the chapter I've dealt with polenta. I think this homely food has so much potential served plain, in layers or deep fried. Best of all, it is very easy to make especially now I've discovered a foolproof method.

First, though, I'd like to discuss making your own fresh pasta.

Home-made Pasta

You may wonder, with so much on offer in the shops, whether it is worth making your own. Do! With practice, you can get wonderful light tasty results. You can also add all manner of distinctive flavours. And making your own dough means you can make ravioli which will almost certainly be more lively than anything in the shops.

Pasta-making is fun as long as you have set aside time and got plenty of space in the kitchen. You need lots of room to dry the pasta prior to cooking it, even if you are only making a small quantity of dough.

Like bread-making, the more you make pasta, the easier it becomes. I don't mean to imply that your first attempts are bound to fail, but the more you get used to handling the dough, the thinner you'll be able to roll it and the lighter the end result.

Ingredients: Use a strong flour, such as one recommended for bread-making. This means the dough will roll out more easily. If you use a wholemeal flour, you may need to add more oil to the dough to stop it being dry.

I add eggs to the recipe to make it richer and more stretchy. Soya flour will also enrich the dough, but the result may not be as light and elastic as an egg dough.

Equipment: Pasta dough for lasagne, ravioli and cannelloni has to be rolled out. Use a sturdy rolling-pin, preferably wooden. When you come to cut out sheets of pasta, use a pastry wheel which won't drag the dough out of shape. For ravioli, there are also various gadgets to help you cut neat squares such as a wooden rolling-pin which marks out sections as you roll, or a tray which is sectioned inside.

For other pasta such as ribbons and strings. A small hand-operated pasta machine is a good buy. These act on the principle of a mangle. There are seven settings, each one rolls the dough progressively thinner. In addition there are two cutting sections for tagliatelle and spaghetti. Electric pasta machines are very expensive and probably only worth it if you frequently intend making large quantities.

Pasta Quantities

For fresh pasta, either bought or home-made, you need to allow 100 g (4 oz) fresh pasta per person for a reasonable helping. It is easy to adjust quantities up or down for more or less substantial meals.

If you are using dried pasta allow 75 g (3 oz) per person for a main course.

Storing Pasta

If you make your own pasta, keep it in the fridge and aim to use it in 24 hours. Bought fresh pasta should also be eaten within 24 hours of purchase. Both these products freeze well and can be cooked from frozen.

Dried pasta can be kept at room temperature. It has a shelf-life of several months.

Cooking Pasta

Cook pasta, both fresh or dried, in plenty of boiling salted water, otherwise it has a tendency to stick together and will not cook evenly. I like to add a spoonful of olive oil to the cooking water.

Once cooked, pasta should be eaten straightaway. Try to remember to have warm plates ready.

Basic Egg Pasta

MAKES enough pasta for 3–4 as a light main course

350 g (12 oz) strong white flour
1 teaspoon salt
3 large eggs
Olive oil if needed

Mix the flour and salt. Make a well in the centre and break in the eggs. Use a knife to mix the flour and eggs together to make a dough. If the mixture is too dry, add equal quantities of olive oil and water about 1 teaspoon at a time until you have a smooth dough. Knead for about 2 minutes.

Cover with cling film and leave to rest for about 30 minutes.

Roll out as thinly as possible for lasagne or ravioli, or put the dough through pasta machine for tagliatelle, spaghetti etc. Leave the hand- or machine-rolled dough to dry out on a lightly floured surface or tea towel for about an hour before cooking.

Once the dough has dried out sufficiently so that the pieces no longer stick to each other, they can be wrapped in cling film and stored for 24 hours in the fridge, or frozen.

Flavoured and Coloured Pasta

It is best to be fairly well-practised with a basic dough before making variations. Additions will invariably alter the look and texture of the dough so you have to be confident that you are going to get it right in the first place. Add dry flavourings to the flour before adding the eggs.

Herb pasta: add 25–50 g (1–2 oz) very finely chopped fresh parsley or basil to the basic mixture. This will give attractive green flecks.

Buckwheat pasta: substitute half the white flour for buckwheat flour. This works well with spicy sauces and mushroom flavours.

Baby spinach pasta: add 50 g (2 oz) very finely chopped raw spinach. This flecks the pasta green.

Sun-dried tomato pasta: add 1–2 tablespoons very finely chopped pieces of sun-dried tomatoes or sun-dried tomato paste to the basic mixture. This gives you a reddish pasta as the tomatoes seem to add colour to the whole dough.

Tomato and Fresh Herb Sauce

Strands of pasta such as tagliatelle, linguine, fettucine as well as spirals, bows and shells all go with an enormous variety of sauces. I've started my suggestions with a simple tomato sauce, one of the main ingredients of which is passata.

Passata is sometimes sold as 'creamed tomatoes'. However, passata is made from sieved creamed tomatoes. Its consistency is smooth. It looks stronger than tinned tomatoes but they are the same strength. Passata has a smoother flavour and undoubtedly a better texture. Although it is mostly sold in packets, tins and jars of passata are also available.

MAKES enough for 450 g (1 lb fresh pasta)

1 tablespoon olive oil
1 onion, chopped
2 cloves garlic, peeled and crushed
1 red pepper, de-seeded and chopped
450 g (1 lb) passata
6 sun-dried tomatoes (in oil)

2 tablespoons chopped fresh basil
2 tablespoons chopped fresh oregano
½ teaspoon ground cinnamon
Salt and freshly ground black pepper

Heat the oil and fry the onion and garlic until soft but not coloured. Using a processor or blender, purée the red pepper with both types of tomatoes and the fresh herbs. Pour this mixture onto the onions, add the cinnamon and stir well. Bring the mixture to the boil, then simmer for 30–40 minutes over a low heat. Season to taste.

Roasted Pepper and Fennel Sauce

Roasted peppers add a sweet caramel flavour to this sauce which is well balanced by the aniseed taste of fennel. This sauce is a good partner to egg pasta such as farfalle, little bows or pasta shells.

PREVIOUS PAGES
Left: Farfalle with *Roasted Pepper and Fennel Sauce*
Right: *Spinach Linguine with Tomato, Dill and Parmesan Sauce* (page 126)

Makes enough for 450 g (1 lb) fresh pasta

1 red pepper
1 yellow pepper
2 tablespoons olive oil
1 onion, chopped
1 clove garlic, peeled and
    crushed
1 bulb fennel, chopped
2 courgettes, diced

450 g (1 lb) passata (page 124)
1 tablespoon sun-dried tomato
    paste
1 bay leaf
2 teaspoons chopped fresh
    oregano
Salt and freshly ground black
    pepper

Pre-heat the oven to 200°C/400°F/gas 6.

Brush the peppers with a little oil, then bake for 30 minutes or until the skin is charred. Leave to cool, peel, remove the seeds and chop well.

Heat the oil and gently cook the onion and garlic until soft. Add the fennel and courgettes and cook for 5 minutes. Then add the chopped peppers. Pour over the passata and add the sun-dried tomato paste and herbs. Bring the mixture to the boil and simmer for 40–45 minutes. Season to taste.

Fusilli and Flageolet with Thyme and Basil

Pecorino is a hard, grating cheese, similar to Parmesan but made
traditionally from ewe's milk. It has a shorter maturing time than
Parmesan, about 8 months. It is consequently a little more moist, and a
fraction milder. I particularly like it with vegetable sauces
such as in this recipe.

Serves 4

1 onion, chopped
2 cloves garlic, peeled and
    crushed
2 tablespoons olive oil
4 sticks celery, chopped
1 × 400 g (14 oz) tin flageolet
    beans
2 tablespoons chopped fresh
    basil

1 teaspoon chopped fresh thyme
400 g (14 oz) passata
    (see page 124)
2 tablespoons sun-dried tomato
    paste
Salt and freshly ground black
    paper
450 g (1 lb) fresh egg fusilli
Freshly grated pecorino to serve

Sweat the onion and garlic in the oil until soft, then add the celery and cook for 3–4 minutes. Add the beans, herbs, passata and sun-dried tomato paste. Bring to the boil and simmer for 20 minutes. Season well.

Cook the fusilli in plenty of boiling, salted water. Drain well and toss into the sauce. Serve on hot plates with freshly grated pecorino.

Spinach Linguine with Tomato, Dill and Parmesan Sauce

This smooth sauce enriched with cream and a hint of dill works well, colourwise, with a spinach pasta such as linguine or paglia e fieno.

SERVES 4

2 tablespoons olive oil
1 large onion, finely chopped
2 cloves garlic, peeled and
    crushed
450 g (1 lb) passata (page 124)
300 ml (10 fl oz) single cream

50 g (2 oz) fresh Parmesan,
    grated
2 tablespoons chopped fresh dill
Salt and freshly ground black
    pepper
450 g (1 lb) fresh pasta

To garnish

Black olives, unpitted
Freshly grated Parmesan

Heat the oil and fry the onion and garlic slowly until very soft. Add the passata and bring to the boil, then simmer for 20 minutes. Leave to cool then blend until smooth. Stir in the cream, Parmesan and dill. Blend briefly until smooth. Season to taste and gently re-heat.

Meanwhile cook the pasta in plenty of boiling, salted water. Drain well and serve on warm plates topped with the sauce. Garnish with black olives and Parmesan.

Tomato Tagliatelle with Broccoli and Mushroom Sauce

Time the cooking of the pasta to be ready as soon as the broccoli is cooked as otherwise its brightness will be lost. This sauce looks good with a tomato-coloured pasta such as tagliatelle.

SERVES 4

1 onion, finely chopped
2 cloves garlic, peeled and
    crushed
50 g (2 oz) butter
100 g (4 oz) mushrooms, sliced
120 ml (4 fl oz) white wine
15 g (½ oz) plain flour

300 ml (10 fl oz) milk
4 tablespoons single cream
Salt and freshly ground black
    pepper
225 g (8 oz) broccoli florets
450 g (1 lb) fresh pasta

Sweat the onion and garlic in the butter for several minutes. Add the mushrooms and cook until tender. Pour over the wine and boil for 4 minutes. Sprinkle in the flour and cook for 2–3 minutes. Then add the milk and stir well until boiling. Simmer for 3 minutes. Stir in the cream and season to taste.

Meanwhile steam the broccoli florets until tender. Stir these into the mushroom sauce. Cook the pasta in plenty of boiling, salted water. Drain and serve on warm plates topped with sauce.

Lemon Basil Butter

Pasta does not always have to be accompanied by a full-blown sauce as this and the next recipe shows. Both ideas are quick to prepare, and yet despite the lack of liquid as in a sauce, the pasta is still moist to eat.

This flavoured butter must be one of the simplest ways to serve pasta. It is very light and tasty and works well as a starter or light main course.

MAKES enough for 450 g (1 lb) pasta

100 g (4 oz) butter
6 tablespoons chopped fresh
basil
2 cloves garlic, peeled and
crushed
2 tablespoons lemon juice
Freshly ground black pepper

Cream the butter. Then cream again with the basil, garlic and lemon juice. Season with black pepper. Chill.

Toss into freshly cooked pasta and serve immediately on warm plates.

Oyster Mushroom and Pine Kernel Sauté with Buttered Penne

This flavoursome mixture makes a good first course. Make it into a main course by doubling the quantities and adding some side dishes such as *Roasted Baby Sweetcorn with Rosemary* (page 20) and *Baked Italian Tomatoes with Basil and Balsamic Vinegar* (page 93).

25 g (1 oz) pine kernels
4 tablespoons olive oil
275 g (10 oz) oyster mushrooms,
  sliced
2 cloves garlic, peeled and
  crushed
Salt and freshly ground black
  pepper
125–175 g (4–6 oz) penne or
  pasta shells

15–25 g (½–1 oz) butter
3–4 tablespoons finely chopped
  flatleaf parsley
2 teaspoons chopped fresh
  marjoram
Freshly grated Parmesan
  shavings to serve

Pre-heat the oven to 200°C/400°F/gas 6.

Roast the pine kernels for 3–4 minutes on a baking tray.

Heat the oil and fry the mushrooms and garlic on a high heat until well browned. Season well and add the pine kernels and fry for a few minutes more.

Cook the pasta in plenty of boiling, salted water until just tender. Drain and toss in the butter, then toss in the cooked mushroom mixture. Spoon the mixture onto warm plates, sprinkle over the parsley, marjoram and Parmesan shavings and serve immediately.

Ravioli with Toasted Pine Kernels and Ricotta

Ravioli filling needs to have plenty of flavour and a moist but not sloppy texture. Spinach and mushrooms are popular ingredients, but do cook them thoroughly and drain well. I like this easy herb and cheese filling flavoured with roasted pine kernels.

To serve the cooked ravioli, you can use melted butter and Parmesan cheese. Try the *Lemon Basil Butter* (page 127), the *Tomato and Fresh Herb Sauce* on page 124 or make a simple tomato sauce.

4–5 tablespoons pesto
40 g (1½ oz) toasted pine
  kernels, ground
75 g (3 oz) ricotta

Salt and freshly ground black
  pepper
1 quantity Basic Egg Pasta
  (see page 121)
1 egg, beaten

Blend the pesto, pine kernels and ricotta using a small nut mill or blender to make a smooth filling. Season to taste.

Roll the pasta dough out very thinly into a large sheet. Divide in half and mark one piece into 72 squares. Place ⅓–½ teaspoon of filling in the middle of each square. Brush the spaces in between with beaten egg. Cover with the remaining pasta. Press firmly around the filling and cut into squares. Leave to dry for an hour before cooking.

To cook, have ready a very large pan of boiling, salted water and cook the ravioli for about 5–6 minutes. Drain very well. Toss in a little butter if you wish, then serve immediately on hot plates with your chosen sauce.

Lasagne

There are an enormous number of possibilities with lasagne. One of today's time-savers is fresh lasagne. This only needs to be covered in boiling water, then drained and it is ready to use. A quick alternative is no-cook lasagne, which you use straight from the box. Just a word of advice. Don't overlap the pieces as they won't cook properly. If you want to use more pasta, make a separate layer.

Here are two recipes – a mushroom lasagne with fresh plum tomatoes and a walnut pesto and a summer lasagne with goat's cheese, wine and more than a hint of marjoram.

Lasagne with Mushrooms and Pesto

SERVES 4

For the mushroom sauce

2 tablespoons olive oil
1 onion, chopped
2 cloves garlic, peeled and
    crushed
450 g (1 lb) mushrooms, sliced

450 g (1 lb) fresh plum
    tomatoes
2 tablespoons pesto
Salt and freshly ground black
    pepper

For the béchamel

450 ml (15 fl oz) milk
6 black peppercorns
¼ onion
1 bay leaf

Sprig of thyme
40 g (1½ oz) butter
25 g (1 oz) plain flour

6 sheets fresh lasagne
Freshly grated Parmesan

Heat the oil and gently cook the onion and garlic. Add the mushrooms and cook until fairly soft.

Cover the tomatoes with boiling water, then peel and chop roughly, add to the pan with the pesto. Cook the mixture for at least 20 minutes. Season to taste.

To make the béchamel sauce, warm the milk and add the peppercorns, onion, bay leaf and thyme. Leave to infuse for 15 minutes. Melt the butter, add the flour and cook over a gentle heat for 2 minutes. Strain the milk and add this to the roux. Bring to the boil, stirring constantly and simmer for 2–3 minutes until the sauce thickens.

Soak the fresh lasagne in boiling water for 3 minutes. Drain and separate the sheets.

Pre-heat the oven to 200°C/400°F/gas 6.

To assemble the dish, place 2–3 spoonfuls of mushroom sauce on the bottom of a large ovenproof dish, cover with 2 sheets of lasagne. Cover these with half the mushroom sauce and a little béchamel sauce. Repeat finishing with sheets of lasagne. Cover these with the remaining béchamel sauce and top with grated Parmesan. Bake for 35–40 minutes or until browned on the top.

Lasagne with Summer Vegetables and Marjoram Sauce

In this recipe I've used goat's cheese to give a tang to the béchamel. Choose a fresh soft goat's cheese with a mild flavour.

SERVES 4

For the vegetable sauce

4 tablespoons olive oil
1 onion, chopped
2 cloves garlic, peeled and
    crushed
50 ml (2 fl oz) white wine

450 g (1 lb) courgettes
450 g (1 lb) plum tomatoes,
    peeled and chopped
1 tablespoon chopped fresh
    marjoram

PREVIOUS PAGES
Left: Fusilli with Lemon Basil Butter (page 127)
Right: Lasagne with Summer Vegetables and
Marjoram Sauce

For the béchamel

450 ml (15 fl oz) milk
6 black peppercorns
¼ onion
1 bay leaf
Sprig of thyme

40 g (1½ oz) butter
25 g (1 oz) plain flour
175 g (6 oz) fresh goat's cheese
Salt and freshly ground black
    pepper

6 sheets fresh lasagne
Freshly grated Parmesan

Heat the oil and gently cook the onion and garlic. Add the wine and cook for 10 minutes or until the liquid has reduced. Add the courgettes, tomatoes and marjoram and bring to the boil. Simmer, covered, for 20 minutes.

To make the béchamel, warm the milk and add the peppercorns, onion, bay leaf and thyme. Leave to infuse for 15 minutes. Melt the butter, add the flour and cook over a gentle heat for 2 minutes. Strain the milk and add this to the roux. Bring to the boil, stirring constantly, and simmer for 2–3 minutes until the sauce thickens.

Mix the goat's cheese into a third of the béchamel sauce and adjust the seasoning.

Cover the lasagne with boiling water for 3 minutes. Drain and separate the sheets.

Pre-heat the oven to 200°C/400°F/gas 6.

To assemble the dish, place 2–3 spoonfuls of the vegetable sauce on the bottom of a large ovenproof dish, cover with 2 sheets of lasagne. Cover with half the vegetable sauce and half of the goat's cheese sauce. Repeat using the other half of the goat's cheese sauce, finishing with sheets of lasagne. Cover these with the remaining béchamel sauce and top with grated Parmesan. Bake for 35–40 minutes or until browned on the top.

Polenta

Don't think of polenta as leaden and worthy. These golden cubes with their dry tang of cornbread are lightly textured. Once cooked, polenta is best heated through in a sauce. Each cube melts to the consistency of a savoury custard. Polenta marries well with most of the sauces I've suggested for pasta on pages 124–32.

Deep-fried polenta is equally, if not more, delicious – crisply coated squares with a melting inside. Serve it as a starter with a hot relish, salsa or tapenade.

Polenta is a flour made from maize or corn. Confusingly there are several grades of flour sold. You need a coarse flour. It may be sold as maize meal or corn flour or, if you are lucky, polenta. You should not buy the sort of cornflour that thickens sauces.

Cooking Polenta

The microwave has revolutionized the cooking of polenta. No more splattering saucepans of yellow porridge that needs an ever-watchful eye. Simply put the whole lot in a large bowl, plus water and a cover, press the timer and you're away.

Instructions for microwave and conventional cookery are given below, along with baked polenta recipes, instructions on how to deep-fry it plus a couple of ideas for dips.

Basic Polenta

SERVES 4

200 g (7 oz) coarse polenta
1.2 litres (2 pints) boiling water
1 teaspoon salt
50 g (2 oz) margarine

To cook the polenta in the microwave: put it in a large bowl. Pour over the boiling water. Add the salt and stir well. Cook the polenta for 8–10 minutes on high heat, stirring at least twice during cooking. Remove from the microwave and beat in the margarine and pour the mixture into a greased dish about 20 × 20 cm (8 × 8 inches). Leave to cool. Turn the cold polenta out on to a chopping board or flat surface and cut into bite-sized squares.

To cook the polenta in the conventional way: using a large pan bring the water and salt to the boil. Pour in the polenta, stirring the whole time, until the mixture is very smooth. Simmer the polenta for 20–30 minutes. Stir frequently to prevent the mixture catching on the base of the pan. Off the heat, stir in the margarine and pour the mixture into a greased dish about 20 × 20 cm (8 × 8 inches). Leave to cool. Turn the cold polenta out on to a chopping board or flat surface and cut into bite-sized squares.

Polenta with Lancashire Cheese
and Sage Sauce

Lancashire cheese has a sharp flavour and crumbly texture. It goes well with sage to make this full-flavoured sauce for polenta.

SERVES 4

1 quantity of Basic Polenta
(see page 134)
50 g (2 oz) Lancashire cheese,
crumbled or grated

For the sauce

40 g (1½ oz) butter
1 shallot, chopped
40 g (1½ oz) plain flour
450 ml (15 fl oz) infused milk
(see page 133)
1 tablespoon chopped fresh
parsley

1 teaspoon chopped fresh sage
4 teaspoons lemon juice
½ teaspoon Dijon mustard
Salt and freshly ground black
pepper
Extra Lancashire cheese to finish
Fresh sage leaves to garnish

Prepare the polenta by cooking it either in the microwave or by the conventional method described on page 134. Add the Lancashire cheese when you beat in the margarine.

For the sauce, melt the butter and gently cook the shallot. Add the flour and cook for 2 minutes. Pour over the flavoured milk, add the parsley and, stirring all the time, bring to the boil and simmer. Add the lemon juice and mustard and season to taste.

Pre-heat the oven to 190°C/375°F/gas 5.

To finish the dish, place the polenta cubes in an ovenproof dish, pour over the sauce, sprinkle on extra Lancashire cheese and heat through in the oven for 15–20 minutes. Garnish with fresh sage leaves.

Polenta with Artichoke and Caper Sauce

This colourful mixture, pungent with herbs looks wonderful poured over the golden cubes of polenta. The mozzarella makes a melting tender topping.

SERVES 4

1 quantity of Basic Polenta
(see page 134)
2 tablespoons olive oil
1 onion
2 cloves garlic
1 red pepper
1 green pepper
6 artichoke hearts in oil, halved
2–3 teaspoons capers

450 g (1 lb) passata
1 teaspoon chopped fresh thyme
1 teaspoon chopped fresh
oregano
175 g (6 oz) mozzarella
Freshly grated Parmesan
Salt and freshly ground black
pepper

Pre-heat the oven to 190°C/375°F/gas 5.

Prepare the polenta by cooking it either in the microwave or by the conventional method described on page 134.

To make the sauce, heat the oil and gently fry the onion and garlic until soft. Add the red and green peppers, artichoke hearts and capers and cook for a few minutes. Pour over the passata, add the herbs and bring the mixture to the boil. Simmer for 35–40 minutes. Season well.

Put a little sauce in the bottom of a shallow dish (or in individual dishes). Then add the cubes of polenta and slices of mozzarella. Top with the remaining sauce. Dust with Parmesan cheese, season to taste and bake for 30–35 minutes or until very hot. Serve immediately.

Deep-fried Polenta

Deep-fried polenta goes well with all manner of dips. Go for colour contrasts as well as flavour. I particularly like the two in the next recipes, one red and fiery, the other pungent and purple black. You could also make *Guacamole* (page 197) or *Roasted Tomato and Chilli Coulis* (page 220).

SERVES 4

1 quantity Basic Polenta (see page 134)	*25 g (1 oz) fine corn meal*
1 egg, beaten	*Oil for frying*

Dip each polenta square into beaten egg then coat well with fine corn meal. Heat the oil in a wide pan or deepfryer and fry the cubes of polenta until well browned and crisp on the outside. The inside should be meltingly soft. Serve hot with an appropriate dip.

Spiced Pepper Coulis

SERVES 4

2 red peppers	*1 clove garlic, peeled and crushed*
1 fresh red chilli, finely chopped	*1 teaspoon caster sugar*
1 red onion, chopped	*Juice of ½ lime*
2 tablespoons olive oil or Chilli Oil (see page 80)	*Salt and freshly ground black pepper*
1 tablespoon chopped sun-dried tomatoes (in oil)	

Pre-heat the oven to 200°C/400°F/gas 6.

Roast the peppers for 30–35 minutes. Leave to cool and then peel off the skin and remove the seeds. Chop finely. Put all the ingredients except the lime juice and seasoning in a saucepan and simmer for 30 minutes or until the ingredients are well cooked to a pulp. Cool and roughly purée in a blender or processor. Add the lime juice and season to taste.

Marinated Olive Tapenade

For a full flavour, use marinated olives (your own or shop-bought). Plain olives will do but you may want to use extra herbs. Fresh herbs give the tapenade a better flavour. Alter the quantities to suit your taste.

SERVES 4

100 g (4 oz) Marinated Olives
(see page 78)
1 clove garlic, peeled and crushed
2 tablespoons lemon juice
2 teaspoons lemon zest
1 tablespoon capers
3–4 tablespoons olive oil
1–2 teaspoons chopped fresh
thyme
1–2 teaspoons chopped fresh
oregano
1 tablespoon chopped fresh basil
Salt and freshly ground black
pepper

Put all the ingredients in a food processor or blender and blend until smooth. Leave to stand for several hours before serving.

OVERLEAF
Left: *Polenta with Artichoke and Caper Sauce* (page 135);
background left: *Marinated Olive Tapenade*;
background right: *Spiced Pepper Coulis* (page 136)
and foreground: *Deep-fried Polenta* (page 136)

RICE

I have switched allegiances.

I spent the first few years of my wholefood shop-owning career extolling the merits of brown rice. I still believe that it wins hands down when it comes to any competition between ordinary white and ordinary brown. I emphasize the word 'ordinary' to distinguish these rices from the many specialist rices now on sale. These 'new' rices have done much to reinstate rice as a fashionable grain, and certainly one worth writing a recipe or two for.

I am now a complete convert to basmati rice, both white and brown, for pilau or pilaf and as an all-round accompaniment. As for risottos, I adore the smooth creamy texture of the Italian risotto rices.

It's amazing to find there are some 7000 different varieties of rice around the world. These fall into roughly a dozen distinct types, each favoured by a different cuisine. The length and thickness of the grain, the amount of starch it contains, and the method of cooking all influence the finished result.

Ultimately the choice of rice for each dish remains personal. Basmati rice and long-grain (brown and white), will interchange happily, but you might miss out on that special fragrance. It is possible to make risotto from a brown short-grain: the recipe will still work, but you can never achieve the authentic consistency. So, if your stock of rice consists of one brand, do make room for a few more. A specialist rice can make all the difference.

Buying and Storing Rice

Whilst rice does have a long shelf-life it is worth buying it from a place with a high turnover so that at least it is fresh when it gets to you. Supermarkets usually have a choice of plain long-grain, basmati and a risotto rice. Wholefood shops are the best bet for a brown basmati, and Italian shops may give you a choice of risotto rice.

Store rice in a cool, dry place and it shouldn't deteriorate. If you buy a cardboard box of rice, it is worth transferring this into an air-tight container. Aim to use rice within the year. If you do end up having half a dozen special rices in your cupboard you should be able to use them all up in this time.

Cooking Rice

There are several methods of cooking rice as a plain accompaniment: open pan, that is using lots of water and draining at the end; closed pan, using a specific amount of water that should be absorbed by the time the rice is cooked; and using the microwave. Follow the instructions on the packet for whichever method you choose. Do not mix metric and imperial methods. In the following recipes, I have included detailed instructions which are specific to each recipe rather than describe it all here.

Basmati Rice

I've been completely won over by basmati rice with its fragrant scent and light fluffy grains. I'll even abandon wholefood instincts and admit that the white variety is just as declicious as the brown. I regard brown and white basmati rice as interchangeable.

Basmati rice, rightfully called the 'King of Rices', is a slender long-grain rice grown in the foothills of the Himalayas. As it cooks it gives off a fragrance which permeates the house. Once cooked the grains will separate easily, fluff them up with a fork. This rice is used traditionally in pilaf and biryani. Cooked plainly it can accompany virtually any dish from stew to stir-fry.

Simple Fragrant Rice

The fragrance in this rice dish comes from both the smell of the basmati rice as it cooks but also from the addition of mild spices. 225 g (8 oz) rice is generally recommended as sufficient for 4. Simply increase the quantities if you have a hungry family. I generally do! Use this rice as an accompaniment to stir-fried vegetable dishes or casseroles.

SERVES 4

2 tablespoons sunflower oil
1 small onion, finely chopped
1 clove garlic, peeled and crushed
1 teaspoon ground cinnamon
1 bay leaf

6 cloves
225 g (8 oz) white basmati rice
600 ml (1 pint) boiling water
Salt and freshly ground black
    pepper

Heat the oil and gently fry the onion and garlic until quite soft. Add the cinnamon, bay leaf and cloves and cook for a minute or so, then add the rice and the boiling water with salt to taste. Bring to the boil, stir once or twice, then cover the pan and simmer for 12 minutes or until rice is tender. Season to taste, fluff up with a fork and serve.

Minted Pilau with Peas and Pine Kernels

I make many versions of pilau or pilaf, the classic one-pot rice dish. This mildly spiced recipe has peas and pine kernels to add texture and colour. Adding mint at the last moment lifts the flavours as well as giving the rice a pretty green hue. Serve this with *Garlic and Coriander Nan* (page 189), *Spiced Peanut Dhal* (page 161) and *Spiced Okra and Potato* (page 59) for a substantial supper.

SERVES 4

2 tablespoons sunflower oil
½ teaspoon cumin seeds
1–2 fresh green chillies,
    de-seeded and finely
    chopped
1 teaspoon garam masala
½ teaspoon ground
    coriander
½ teaspoon turmeric
1 onion, finely chopped

3 cloves garlic, peeled and
    crushed
225 g (8 oz) frozen peas
50 g (2 oz) pine kernels
225 g (8 oz) brown basmati rice
600 ml (1 pint) boiling water
2 tablespoons chopped fresh
    mint
Salt and freshly ground black
    pepper

Heat the oil and add the cumin seeds and chilli and cook for 3 minutes. Add the garam masala, coriander and turmeric, cook for 1 minute, then add the onion and garlic and cook for 5 minutes. Add the peas and pine kernels and rice and stir well. Pour over the boiling water. Bring to the boil and cook for 20 minutes. The rice should be tender. If there is excess water, leave the lid off the pan and let the excess reduce. Mix in the mint and adjust the seasoning. Serve hot.

Chinese White Glutinous Rice

This is also known as sticky rice. It is a variety of rice with round, pearl-like grains which have a slightly sweet flavour once cooked. Despite its name, this rice is gluten-free. Its stickiness comes from a combination of its high starch content and softness of the grain. When cooked the grains will hold together easily, making it an ideal rice for rice balls or savoury stuffings.

Sushi Rolls

Chinese glutinous rice makes a traditional sticky filling for these bite-sized rolls. There are several methods for cooking this rice, either in boiling water until it reaches the right consistency or in a double boiler. It is traditional to fan the rice until it's cool. It is important to wash the rice several times before cooking it. (If you cannot get this rice, use a risotto rice, though it won't be quite the same.) The rice is served rolled up in a sheet of nori, a type of seaweed. The nori needs toasting first as I've explained in the recipe. Special nori for sushi rolls is available in specialist shops. This is pre-toasted and called sushi nori.

These sushi rolls are served cold, so make sure the filling is well flavoured. You can add small pieces of raw carrot, cucumber, spring onions or pickled walnuts or gherkins.

SERVES 4–6

*175 g (6 oz) Chinese glutinous
    rice
1 clove garlic, peeled and crushed
1 × 1 cm (½ inch) piece root
    ginger, peeled and grated
1 tablespoon rice vinegar or cider
    vinegar
½ teaspoon creamed horseradish
Salt and freshly ground black
    pepper
3 sheets nori (see above)
3 tablespoons shoyu*

Wash the rice several times, then soak in hot water for a couple of hours. Have ready a large pan of boiling water, then add the rice and its soaking water, bring to the boil and simmer for 10–12 minutes. If it is not very sticky, cook until it is thick and sticky. Drain if necessary. Turn into a large bowl and cool quickly, then stir in the garlic, ginger, vinegar and horseradish. Season to taste.

Take 1 sheet of nori and pass it over a flame until it turns green. (If using sushi nori, this step isn't necessary.) Brush the nori with 1 tablespoon shoyu. Put 8 tablespoons rice mixture onto the nori sheet and spread it over the sheet evenly using wet hands. Roll up tightly, then trim the ends with a knife. Cut into 8 pieces. Repeat with the other sheets.

Long-grain Brown Rice

Compared to some of the previous glamorous descriptions of rice, it's tricky to make plain long-grain sound much more than an also-ran. I'm aware that even saying it is good for you makes it sound worthy and dull. Well it is good for you! It has a nutty flavour with a pleasant spring to the grains which should keep nicely separated once cooked. You can use it instead of basmati to accompany curries or stir-fried dishes. It is equally good with goulashes or stews. If I need a long-grain white rice, I use either basmati or Thai fragrant rice (see page 148).

Pecan Rice with Asparagus Sauce

Toasted pieces of pecan mixed with rice and topped with a delicate pale green sauce make an attractive, simple supper dish. Serve with baby carrots and steamed green beans.

Use either long-grain brown rice, or brown or white basmati rice for this recipe.

SERVES 4

*225 g (8 oz) long-grain brown
rice or basmati rice
2 tablespoons olive oil
2 shallots, finely chopped
100 g (4 oz) shelled pecan nuts,
chopped*

For the sauce

1 bunch asparagus
25 g (1 oz) butter
2 shallots, finely chopped
2 tablespoons chopped fresh dill

150 ml (5 fl oz) single cream
Salt and fresh ground black
   pepper

Cook the rice in plenty of boiling salted water. Drain when tender. Meanwhile, heat the oil and gently cook the shallots until soft but not coloured. Add the chopped pecan nuts and cook until lightly toasted. Mix the nuts into the cooked rice. Place in a serving dish and keep warm.

For the sauce, trim and then steam the asparagus until tender. This takes 8–10 minutes. Melt the butter and fry the shallots until soft but not coloured. Add the asparagus and cook for a few minutes. Purée the mixture with the dill and cream, and season to taste. Heat gently. Pour over the rice and serve immediately.

Risotto Rice

Italian risotto rice comes from the Po valley. It is a plump robust grain that stands up to a good deal of stirring without breaking down. This makes it ideal for risottos where the method of cooking is to stir the grain almost continually as the water or liquid is absorbed. The high starch content of risotto rice contributes to the final creamy quality.

Risotto rice may be graded as fino and superfino, with the super, as you'd expect, being superior. Arborio is the most widely sold variety. In specialist Italian shops you may also find Carnaroli and Vialone Nano – each has a slightly different texture once cooked.

Almond Risotto with Saffron and Buttered Leeks

A good risotto should be creamy not sticky. It does take time to cook and, unlike most rice dishes, needs lots of attention. But the end result is worth it. Risotto can be served on its own but I like the buttered leeks as a contrasting side dish to make it more of a main meal.

SERVES 4

2 tablespoons olive oil
1 onion, chopped
1 clove garlic, peeled and
     crushed
25 g (1 oz) butter
225 g (8 oz) risotto rice
75 g (3 oz) whole blanched
     almonds, coarsely chopped
150 ml (5 fl oz) white wine

Strands of saffron, loosely piled
     to fill a teaspoon
450 ml (15 fl oz) boiling
     vegetable stock
Salt and freshly ground black
     pepper
15 g (½ oz) butter
25 g (1 oz) freshly grated
     Parmesan

For the leeks

3–4 medium leeks
25 g (1 oz) butter
50 ml (2 fl oz) white wine
2 tablespoons chopped fresh
     flatleaf parsley
Salt and freshly ground black
     pepper

Heat the oil and gently fry the onion and garlic until soft but not coloured. Add the butter to the pan and when melted add the rice and almonds and stir until well coated with butter. Add the wine and cook gently, stirring until the liquid is absorbed, then add the strands of saffron and 150 ml (5 fl oz) stock. Keep stirring and cook until the stock is absorbed and then add a further 150 ml (5 fl oz) and repeat the process before adding the final amount. The rice should become thick and creamy but not sticky. Season to taste. Just before serving add the extra 15 g (½ oz) butter and the Parmesan.

For the leeks, trim them and slice thickly. Melt the butter and gently fry the leeks for 5–8 minutes or until just beginning to soften. Add the wine and bring to the boil. Leave the pan uncovered and simmer the leeks until tender and the liquid has boiled off. Toss in the parsley and seasoning and serve hot with the risotto.

Fennel and Parmesan Risotto

I think this is one of the best ways to eat fennel and, incidentally, rice.
The creamy white purée melts into the rice leaving a subtle
aniseed flavour.

SERVES 4

For the purée

2 tablespoons olive oil
1 onion, chopped
1 clove garlic, peeled and crushed
1 head fennel, trimmed and
    chopped
2 teaspoons walnut oil

For the rice

2 tablespoons olive oil
1 onion, chopped
1 clove garlic, peeled and crushed
225 g (8 oz) risotto rice
600 ml (1 pint) boiling vegetable
    stock
Salt and freshly ground black
    pepper
25 g (1 oz) butter
25 g (1 oz) freshly grated
    Parmesan

First make the fennel purée. Heat the oil and gently cook the onion and garlic so that they are soft but not coloured. Add the fennel and cook slowly for 10 minutes. Then add 300 ml (10 fl oz) water, bring to the boil and cook until the fennel is completely soft. Drain, reserving the liquid. Purée the fennel with the walnut oil, adding a little of the cooking liquid if necessary. Use the remaining cooking liquid to make up the stock needed to cook the rice.

To cook the rice, heat the oil and gently cook the onion and garlic. Add half the butter and when melted add the rice and stir until well coated. Add 150 ml (5 fl oz) boiling stock, stir well and cook until the liquid is almost absorbed. Then add a further 150 ml (5 fl oz). Continue until all the stock is added. Finally stir in the fennel purée. Season to taste and just before serving add the remaining butter and the Parmesan.

Thai Fragrant Rice

This is also sold as jasmine rice. Both delightful names conjure up the aromatic quality of this rice. It has slender long grains, rather like basmati, except they cook to a slightly softer consistency with a milder flavour. Watch this rice towards the end of the recommended cooking time or it can become sticky. It is an ideal rice to serve with oriental or Asian food.

Sweet and Sour Tofu with Rice

Tofu needs strong partners as it will absorb their flavours as it cooks. A sweet and sour sauce is ideal. Keep it plain as in this recipe or add more vegetables. This dish is ideal with Thai fragrant rice or use brown or white basmati.

SERVES 4

1 packet firm tofu
2 tablespoons dry sherry
2 tablespoons shoyu
Freshly ground black pepper

For the sauce

1 tablespoon sunflower oil
3 shallots, finely chopped
2 cloves garlic, peeled and crushed
1 × 1 cm (½ inch) piece root ginger, peeled and grated
225 g (8 oz) cooking apple, peeled and chopped

½ tablespoon cornflour
3 tablespoons water
2 tablespoons cider vinegar
1 tablespoon shoyu
2 tablespoons honey
6 tablespoons passata (page 124)
4 tablespoons fresh orange juice

225 g (8 oz) Thai fragrant rice or basmati rice

Chop the tofu into bite-sized pieces. Mix together the sherry, shoyu and pepper. Marinate the pieces of tofu for at least 30 minutes. Then pre-heat the oven to 200°C/400°F/gas 6. Drain the tofu pieces and bake them on a baking tray for 10 minutes.

For the sauce, heat the oil and gently fry the shallots, garlic and ginger until soft. Then add the apple and cook for 5 minutes. Mix the cornflour with the remaining ingredients. Pour into the pan and bring to the boil so that the sauce thickens and then clears. Add the tofu pieces and cook for 3 minutes.

Cook the rice in double its volume of boiling salted water in a covered pan for 12–15 minutes. Fluff up with a fork and serve with the tofu and sauce.

Wild Rice

Known as the caviar of rice partly because of its black colour, salty tang and horrendously high price. When I first had my shop, I spent nearly a week's takings buying in 2 kilos. Fortunately now, the supermarkets sell it in reasonable quantities such as 100 g (4 oz). Serving wild rice on its own is a waste of money. The long black-brown needles are shown off to better effect against a background of white rice. The flavour of wild rice is strong and will permeate the surrounding grains.

Wild rice grains, which split and curl as they cook, are better if they are slightly chewy rather than soft. I think it is always best to cook wild rice in a separate pan. This method gives you much more control over its cooking time. The alternative is to add another rice to the wild rice at some point during the cooking and hope everything ends up cooked at the same time – not advised!

Wild Rice and Vegetables with Lemon and Ginger Sauce

Wild rice and white rice look marvellous mixed together. Do cook them in separate pans as their cooking times vary considerably. The lemon and ginger sauce is made by infusing spices in boiling water. This is then thickened with cornflour and cooked with the vegetables giving them a spicy tang.

OVERLEAF
Left: *Wild Rice and Vegetables with Lemon and Ginger Sauce*
Right: *Almond Risotto with Saffron and Buttered Leeks* (page 145)

SERVES 4

75 g (3 oz) wild rice
200–225 g (7–8 oz) white
basmati rice

For the sauce

2 small fresh red chillies
1 × 2.5 cm (1 inch) piece root
ginger, peeled and grated
3 sticks fresh lemon grass

2 teaspoons arrowroot
1 tablespoon concentrated apple
juice
1 tablespoon shoyu

For the stir-fry

1 tablespoon sunflower oil
1 clove garlic, peeled and crushed
3 spring onions, chopped
3 sticks celery, sliced
2 yellow peppers, de-seeded and
cut in strips

225 g (8 oz) fine beans, trimmed
and halved
4 tablespoons chopped fresh
coriander

Cook the wild rice in plenty of boiling water for about 45 minutes. Drain and set aside. Cook the white rice in boiling salted water for about 15 minutes. Drain and mix with the wild rice.

Meanwhile prepare the sauce and vegetables. For the sauce, grind the chilli, ginger and lemon grass to a rough paste. Put in a pan with 450 ml (15 fl oz) water, bring to the boil and boil for 10 minutes. Strain and set aside. There should be about 300 ml (10 fl oz) stock.

Dissolve the arrowroot in 1 tablespoon water then pour over the stock and add the concentrated apple juice and shoyu.

For the stir-fry, heat the oil and quickly cook the garlic and spring onions, then add the celery, peppers and fine beans. Keep stirring over a high heat. Pour over the sauce, stirring rapidly and cook for 5–6 minutes or until the sauce is clear and the vegetables just tender. Serve with the rice and garnish with coriander.

SPICES

Spices. Just the word conjures up tantalizing flavours and persuasive aromas.

I'm cheating a little in this book by including a chapter on spices. Most of them are not fresh in either sense of the word. One point of this book though is to help you get the best out of ingredients and prepare them in new ways. For these reasons spices need a mention. Storing and cooking them properly can make all the difference.

As spices tend to work in conjunction with each other, rather than try to link individual spices to one recipe as I did in the herb chapter, I've simply grouped the recipes into two sections: hot, usually those recipes containing chilli and ginger; and mild, recipes that include spices such as coriander, cinnamon and cardamom. Within each section the recipes are then listed alphabetically. I've included notes on buying, storing and using dried spices before the recipes.

Fresh Spices

First I'd like to mention a few of the fresh spices which are a fast-increasing group of ingredients. A few years ago, root ginger was a rare commodity, fresh lemon grass was unheard of. Now these are widely available, as well as a confusing choice of chillies.

Chillies

Scotch Bonnet, Rat Droppings, Birdseye or Habanero are some of the names of chillies you may find in the shops today. Chilli comes in a wide range of strengths from the very mild to the blisteringly hot. As a rough guide, the smaller, narrower and darker the chilli, the more powerful its heat. Thus the tiny spindly Birdseye from Thailand is one to treat with care. Anaheim from America, light green with a long tapering shape, is medium hot to mild. Red chillies are ripe green ones and can taste slightly sweet. (If you leave green chillies to ripen they will become red.) In peak condition all chillies should have a glossy skin. Check there isn't any bruising when buying.

Storing chillies: keep chillies in the fridge and they should last up to three weeks. If they begin to go mouldy separate them out as the mould will spread quickly from one to another. A few fresh chillies can be stored in oil see page 80. Then use the oil for flavouring.

Using chillies: always treat chillies with care. After chopping a chilli (dried or fresh) never touch your eyes or mouth. Wash your hands very thoroughly as well as the chopping board and knife. It is best to err on the side of caution and wear rubber gloves. The seeds and inner membrane are the hottest parts so discard those if you wish.

Chillies can be chopped and added at the beginning of the recipe to infuse the oil. Chillies can also be roasted in the oven, skinned (optional) and added to recipes. This gives the chilli a different taste and is a useful method if making raw relishes.

Start to use chillies cautiously and you will be rewarded. You can create a welcoming underlying warmth up to an intense dramatic heat.

Fenugreek

This is really a herb, though as it is almost always used with spices rather than alone I've included it here. You need to buy fresh fenugreek from an Indian shop. The leaves are small and oval, they have a spicy fragrance and pungent flavour. Use them as soon as possible as fenugreek wilts quickly. Fenugreek seeds make a good alternative – the dried spice has a similar bitter-sweet taste which is released when the seeds are roasted.

Lemon Grass

Lemon grass, pale white to green stems about the size of a pencil, is commonly used in South-east Asian cookery. Lemon grass, as you would expect, adds a light lemon fragrance with a hint of spice. It will keep for two to three weeks in the fridge.

To use, pull off the papery outer leaves. Use whole and remove before serving, or chop and pound to a paste. I have bought freeze-dried lemon grass which looked unpromising but, once soaked, had a good flavour.

Lime Leaves

Fresh lime leaves are dark and glossy and once bruised give a sharp citrus-like scent. Use these leaves whole and remove them before serving. It is useful to let a few leaves dry, then you have them on hand if you haven't got fresh lime.

Root Ginger

One of my favourite gadgets is my ginger grater. Take a gnarled root, peel it and rub it over the grater and instantly there is this spicy pungent juicy flesh. Always buy plump, firm root ginger. It will keep in the fridge for two or three weeks, or even longer though it may begin to dry out. Peel the root before grating or chopping it. Ginger is an essential spice in oriental and West Indian cookery. But don't confine it there. Try it with vegetables such as squash (see *Butternut Squash Soup with Lime and Ginger* on page 54), or with parsnips and carrots. A little raw ginger can also spike up a fresh relish.

Dried Spices

Spices can come from many different parts of a plant or tree. Bark, stem, seeds, and roots and leaves are all used. Unlike herbs which loose the best of their flavour once dried, the drying of spices concentrates and preserves their aromas.

How to Buy and Store Dried Spices

Thanks to the popularity of cuisines such as oriental, Indian, Mexican and Middle Eastern, the range of spices available in supermarkets is now extensive. Sold in small jars, they can be rather pricey. It is sometimes worth searching further even within the same shop. One of my own local supermarkets has another section of spices alongside the rice. Here many spices are sold in 100 g (4 oz) packs and are much better value. Better still, see if you can buy spices loose, that is by the ounce or gram, from a whole-food or ethnic shop.

Spices should be bought whole as opposed to ready ground. Any whole spices, such as coriander seed or cloves, will keep their potency longer. Freshly ground spices are much more aromatic than the ready ground. Quite a good compromise for convenience is to buy small quantities of ground spices that you know you are going to use frequently and buy whole spices, such as cardamom, that you may only use once in a while.

All spices should be kept in air-tight containers in a cool dry place. If kept properly, ground spices should last around 3 months and whole spices up to a year. Do label the jars or tubs clearly. It can be a shock if you add a teaspoon of blisteringly hot cayenne to a dish rather than mild paprika.

How To Use Spices

Spices need to be cooked to release their flavours. Unlike fresh herbs it is usual to add spices at the start of cooking a dish, rather than towards the end.

Spices can be added in two ways to a recipe. First, they can be fried in oil with or before onion or garlic is added. If you are adding ground spices you need to have enough oil to stop the spices burning. As the spices cook, they infuse the oil and this helps to carry the flavour through the dish.

Another method is to roast the spices, whole, then grind them and add to the pan. Roast spices in a dry frying-pan. Keep shaking the pan until the aromas start to be released. The seeds will just darken. Be careful not to scorch them as the taste will then be bitter or burnt. Dry-roasting can also be done in the oven, though you need to keep a constant check.

Roasted spices can be added to the main dish early on in the cooking process. They will infuse the oil in the same way as unroasted spices, but add a different aroma. Roasted spices can also be added to recipes at the end of the cooking. This works well when using spices to flavour an uncooked salsa or relish, or a yoghurt such in *Yoghurt with Cardamom and Pistachio* on page 167.

Hot Dishes

Colourful Pepper Ragout with Coriander and Lime

Mixed packs of peppers are useful for this dish, though you can use just one colour if you prefer. I do think it is worth using fresh tomatoes rather than chopped tinned tomatoes as they are less watery. The success of this dish depends on having a rich pulpy sauce. For a hotter result you can use *Chilli Oil* (see page 80) instead of sunflower oil.

SERVES 4

3 tablespoons sunflower oil
1 onion, finely chopped
2 cloves garlic, peeled and
    crushed
1 fresh green chilli, de-seeded
    and diced
1 red pepper
1 yellow pepper

1 green pepper
450 g (1 lb) fresh tomatoes,
    skinned and roughly chopped
Juice of 1 lime
3–4 tablespoons chopped fresh
    coriander
Salt and freshly ground black
    pepper

Heat the oil and cook the onion, garlic and chilli until fairly soft. Prepare the peppers by removing the seeds and slicing into thin matchsticks. Fry for 3–4 minutes. Add the tomatoes and lime juice. Cook the mixture until the tomatoes have reduced to a thick pulp. Add the fresh coriander, season to taste then serve immediately.

Gujerati Potato Filling for Pancakes

This traditional hot spiced potato dish works well as a filling for pancakes or with filo pastry to make samosa. The sweet spices help to balance the heat of the chilli. Serve these with a plain yoghurt and *Fresh Coriander and Chilli Chutney* (see page 168).

MAKES enough for 8 pancakes

2 tablespoons sunflower oil
1 large carrot, diced
1 large potato, weighing about
    275 g (10 oz), peeled and
    diced
50 g (2 oz) frozen sweetcorn
50 g (2 oz) frozen peas

½ teaspoon salt
Juice of ½ lemon
¼–½ teaspoon chilli powder
1 onion, finely chopped
¼ teaspoon cinnamon
3 cloves, freshly ground
Freshly ground black pepper

Heat the oil and gently fry the carrot and potato, stirring frequently until the vegetables begin to soften. Add the sweetcorn and peas, salt, lemon juice and chilli powder. Continue cooking until the vegetables are quite soft. Next add the onion, cinnamon and cloves and cook until the mixture is quite soft but the onion remains a little crunchy. Season to taste.

Mixed Vegetable Pakora

Gram flour made from chickpeas should be available in larger supermarkets or specialist healthfood shops. I particularly like the banana in this recipe as its texture works well with the root vegetables and the fruity taste contrasts with the floury batter. Pakora are best eaten on the day they are made.

OVERLEAF
Left: *Spiced Beans with Chilli and Cinnamon Salsa* (page 161)
Right: *Colourful Pepper Ragout with Coriander and Lime* (page 156)

SERVES 4

For the batter

90 g (3½ oz) gram flour	*¼ teaspoon sugar*
1 tablespoon oil	*½ teaspoon baking powder*
A pinch of chilli powder	*75 ml (3 fl oz) water*
¼ teaspoon asafoetida	*50 g (2 oz) potato, peeled and*
(see page 59)	*grated*
2 tablespoons chopped fresh	*50 g (2 oz) carrot, grated*
fenugreek or ½ teaspoon	*½ banana, chopped*
crushed fenugreek seeds	*Oil for deep-frying*
¼ teaspoon salt	

To make the batter, mix the gram flour with the oil and all the spices, salt and sugar. Add the baking powder. Then add enough water to make the batter slightly thicker than a pancake batter.

Mix the prepared vegetables and fruit into the batter.

Heat oil (about 5 cm/2 inches in depth) in a small saucepan for deep-frying. Make sure the oil is really hot by dropping in a piece of onion and seeing how quickly it fizzles. Once hot, fry tablespoons of the mixture until lightly brown and crisp. Drain on kitchen paper.

Roasted Peanut Sauce

This classic sauce goes well with plainly cooked vegetables, stir-fried mixtures, pancakes and tortillas.

SERVES 4

100 g (4 oz) unsalted	*1 stick lemon grass, finely chopped*
peanuts	*2 fresh lime leaves*
1 tablespoon sunflower oil	*2 tablespoons lemon juice*
1 onion, finely chopped	*1–2 tablespoons concentrated*
2 cloves garlic, peeled and	*apple juice*
crushed	*Salt and freshly ground black*
2 fresh hot chillies	*pepper*

Pre-heat the oven to 200°C/400°F/gas 6.

Roast the peanuts on a baking tray for 3–4 minutes. Cool and then grind as finely as possible.

Heat the oil and gently cook the onion and garlic until soft. De-seed the chillies and chop them finely. Add these to the pan with the chopped lemon grass, whole lime leaves and ground peanuts. Cook briefly, then add 300 ml (10 fl oz) water. Stir well and add the lemon juice and apple juice to taste. Bring to the boil and simmer gently for 35–40 minutes, stirring frequently.

Cool slightly, remove the lime leaves then purée until smooth. Add extra liquid if necessary. Season to taste and re-heat before serving.

Spiced Beans with Chilli and Cinnamon Salsa

This simple dish, quick to make and full of flavour, can be part of a main course, served as a side vegetable or used to fill shop-bought tortillas.

SERVES 4

1 hot fresh green chilli
1 small onion, chopped
1 clove garlic, peeled and chopped
½ teaspoon ground cinnamon
150 ml (5 fl oz) passata
  (page 124)

Salt and freshly ground black
  pepper
1 × 400 g (14 oz) tin mixed
  beans
150 ml (5 fl oz) soured cream to
  serve

Pre-heat the oven to 200°C/400°F/gas 6.

Split the chilli and remove the seeds. Then bake it for 10 minutes. Cool and peel off the skin.

Process the chilli with the onion, garlic, cinnamon and passata to make a smooth sauce. Season to taste.

Put the beans in a saucepan and add the sauce. Then gently heat through. Serve with the soured cream.

Spiced Peanut Dhal

The long list of ingredients may be daunting but it is mostly a selection of spices which give this soup a wonderful warm flavour. It is a meal in itself especially if accompanied by nan bread (see *Garlic and Coriander Nan* on page 189).

SERVES 4

75 g (3 oz) yellow split peas
900 ml (1½ pints) water
2 tablespoons sunflower oil
1 large carrot (weighing about
   100 g/4 oz), diced
1 large potato (weighing about
   225 g/8 oz), peeled and
   diced
100 g (4 oz) frozen peas
1 small onion chopped
50 g (2 oz) unsalted peanuts
¼ teaspoon chilli powder
½ teaspoon turmeric
½ teaspoon black mustard seeds,
   ground

½ teaspoon fenugreek seeds,
   ground
1 × 400 g (14 oz) tin chopped
   tomatoes
1 tablespoon tomato purée
1 × 1 cm (½ inch) piece of root
   ginger, peeled and grated
Juice of ½ lemon
1 teaspoon sugar
¼ teaspoon coriander seeds
3 cloves
2–3 tablespoons chopped fresh
   coriander
Salt and freshly ground black
   pepper

Bring the yellow split peas to the boil in the water then simmer until completely soft. Drain, reserving the stock.

In a large pan, heat the oil and fry the carrot, potato, peas, onion and peanuts. Sprinkle over the chilli powder, turmeric, mustard and fenugreek. Cook the vegetables until fairly soft, stirring frequently. Add the chopped tomatoes, tomato purée, ginger and lemon juice, sugar, cooked yellow split peas and about 600 ml (1 pint) stock. Add more stock if necessary. Simmer for 30–40 minutes.

In a dry frying-pan, toast the coriander seeds and cloves. Grind finely then add to the soup with the fresh coriander. Season to taste.

Spiced Sesame and Shoyu Dip

This is a useful dip for raw vegetables, spring rolls or baked tofu pieces
(see page 148).

1 × 2.5 cm (1 inch) piece root
   ginger, peeled and crushed
2 cloves garlic, peeled and
   crushed

2 spring onions, diced
4 tablespoons sesame oil
Shoyu to taste
Freshly ground black pepper

Mix the ginger, garlic and spring onions in a bowl. Heat the oil and pour over these ingredients and leave to cool. Add shoyu and pepper to taste.

Spring Rolls with Ginger Soy Sauce

I find it easier to bake rather than fry spring rolls. I brush them with oil which makes them quite crisp and dry. Once cooked it is good to serve them with a dipping sauce. Miniature spring rolls make a good savoury to hand round before a meal.

SERVES 4

1 packet firm tofu

For the marinade

2 tablespoons shoyu
2 tablespoons water
1 tablespoon dry sherry
1 tablespoon freshly grated root ginger

1 tablespoon sesame oil
2 cloves garlic, peeled and crushed
1 teaspoon brown sugar

For the filling

1 tablespoon peanut or sunflower oil
6 spring onions, chopped
1 clove garlic, peeled and chopped
100 g (4 oz) beansprouts

1 large carrot, diced
Salt and freshly ground black pepper
8 sheets filo pastry (see page 47)
Oil for brushing

Chop the tofu into small pieces. Mix together all the ingredients for the marinade, place the tofu in the mixture and leave to marinate for at least 2 hours, turning the pieces over occasionally. Drain well, reserving the marinade.

Heat the oil and quickly fry the spring onions and garlic, then add the beansprouts, carrot and tofu. Cook until the carrots are just beginning to soften. Season the mixture.

Pre-heat the oven to 200°C/400°F/gas 6. Brush the sheets of filo well with oil. Fold in the edges, fill with an eighth of the mixture and roll up, brushing again with oil. Place the filled rolls on an oiled baking sheet or parchment. Bake for 15–18 minutes.

Serve warm with the remaining marinade poured over the top or served separately as a dipping sauce.

Milder Dishes

Aromatic Couscous

Couscous, derived from wheat, looks like hundreds of tiny pale gold balls. Traditionally couscous is placed in a fine sieve and steamed over a stew. Once cooked it has a very soft texture which works well with contrasting chunky vegetable pieces. Cooking couscous in the microwave makes it very quick. You must be careful not to cook it to the consistency of baby food, and secondly choose a container big enough so that the couscous doesn't splatter everywhere. Microwaving is especially useful if you want to prepare this stew well ahead.

SERVES 4

4 tablespoons olive oil
1 onion, chopped
1 teaspoon ground coriander
¼ teaspoon allspice
¼ teaspoon turmeric
¼ teaspoon ground ginger
350 g (12 oz) butternut squash, cut into cubes
350 g (12 oz) carrots, peeled and sliced

1 × 400 g (14 oz) tin chick peas, drained
100 g (4 oz) raisins
1 × 400 g (14 oz) tin chopped tomatoes
Salt and freshly ground black pepper
225 g (8 oz) couscous

Heat the oil and fry the onion for several minutes. Add the spices and fry for a few minutes. Add the vegetables and chick peas and cook very slowly until just beginning to soften. Stir in the raisins and then add the tin of tomatoes and bring the mixture to the boil. Simmer gently for at least an hour. Season well.

If you have a fine sieve which fits into the top of the saucepan, place the couscous in it, without touching the liquid below, cover and steam the two together for about 10 minutes or until the couscous is light and fluffy. Season well.

Alternatively cook the couscous in the microwave. Place in a large bowl and pour on 750 ml (1¼ pints) boiling water or vegetable stock. Cook for 3 minutes on high. All the water should be absorbed. Leave to stand for 5 minutes, then fluff up with a fork before serving.

Turn the couscous out on to a large, warmed serving dish and top with the chick pea and vegetable sauce.

Pumpkin Korma

Mild spices such as coriander, cinnamon and cardamom cooked in a yoghurt sauce form the basis of this dish. I've chosen to use pumpkin, but most vegetables can be cooked in this way with the exception of aubergines and mushrooms which turn the sauce grey. Serve this with basmati rice for an easy supper.

SERVES 4

3 tablespoons sunflower oil
1 teaspoon ground coriander
½ teaspoon ground cumin
½ teaspoon ground cardamom
½ teaspoon ground cinnamon
1 onion, chopped
2 cloves garlic, peeled and crushed
300 ml (10 fl oz) set natural yoghurt

1 teaspoon plain flour (optional)
750 g (1½ lb) pumpkin, de-seeded, peeled and diced
1–2 tablespoons fresh lemon juice
Zest of ½ lemon
Salt and freshly ground black pepper
3 tablespoons chopped fresh coriander

Heat the oil and fry the spices for 2–3 minutes. Add the onion and garlic and cook until fairly soft. Add the yoghurt a tablespoon at a time, stirring very well. If the mixture curdles, quickly add the flour. Put in the pumpkin pieces and mix in gently. Cook the mixture over a gentle heat for 30 minutes or until just soft. Add the lemon juice and zest. Season well. Just before serving spinkle over the fresh coriander.

Samosa

I make samosa using filo pastry as, although not traditional, it works very well. Paneer is an Indian curd cheese with quite a dry firm texture. Blocks of paneer are sold by some of the large supermarkets although, frustratingly I have found its supply unreliable. A ricotta cheese makes a reasonable substitute. Remember to make the filling a day in advance for the flavours to develop. Make miniature samosa as a starter, larger ones for lunch-boxes and main meals.

SERVES 4

For the filling

450 g (1 lb) potatoes
175 g (6 oz) frozen peas
2 tablespoons sunflower oil
½ teaspoon cumin seeds
1 teaspoon garam masala
½ teaspoon ground coriander
¼ teaspoon cayenne
1 onion, finely chopped

1 clove garlic, peeled and
    chopped
1 tablespoon fresh lemon
    juice
Salt and freshly ground black
    pepper
100 g (4 oz) paneer or ricotta
    cheese

16 sheets filo pastry
(see page 47)
50–75 g (2–3 oz) butter

Peel the potatoes and boil until tender. Cut in cubes. Cook the peas.

Heat the oil and fry the cumin seeds until lightly toasted, then add the remaining spices and cook for 2 minutes. Add the onion and garlic and cook slowly until the onion is soft. Then add the cooked potato, peas and lemon juice. Cook the mixture for 5 minutes, season to taste and leave to cool, preferably overnight. Stir in the paneer or ricotta cheese.

Pre-heat the oven to 200°C/400°F/gas 6. To make the samosa, brush each sheet of filo pastry with melted butter, fold in half lengthways. Put a spoonful of mixture at one corner, fold over and roll up into a triangle. Then brush again with butter. Repeat with the remaining sheets.

Bake on a baking tray for 15–18 minutes or until the filo is golden brown.

Vegetable Cacerolita
with Cumin and Walnuts

Baked garlic breadcrumbs thicken this stew giving it an almost creamy consistency. I like to make the whole dish well ahead of time so the flavours have a chance to develop.

2 tablespoons olive oil
2 teaspoons cumin seeds
1 onion, chopped
2 cloves garlic, peeled and
  crushed
1 leek, chopped
100 g (4 oz) carrots, chopped
1 green pepper, de-seeded and
  chopped
1 red pepper, de-seeded and
  chopped
225 g (8 oz) tiny button
  mushrooms, halved

12 sun-dried tomatoes (in oil),
  chopped
50 g (2 oz) walnut halves,
  chopped
2 tablespoons red wine
300 ml (10 fl oz) vegetable stock
2 tablespoons passata
  (page 124)
Salt and freshly ground black
  pepper
1 clove garlic, peeled
25 g (1 oz) slice of brown
  bread

Heat the oil and toast the cumin seeds, then add the onion and garlic and cook until soft. Add the vegetables, including the sun-dried tomatoes, and cook slowly for 10 minutes. Next add the walnuts, wine, stock and passata. Bring to the boil and simmer for 45–50 minutes or until the vegetables are soft. Season to taste.

Pre-heat the oven to 180°C/350°F/gas 4. Crush the remaining garlic clove and spread over the bread, then bake it until dry. Grind into breadcrumbs and add to the casserole, stirring in well. Cook a few minutes more before serving.

Yoghurt with Cardamom and Pistachio

The aromatic flavour of cardamom is marvellous with yoghurt. This is a very simple side dish to serve with hot spicy dishes. The flavour of the cardamom seems to take the heat out of some of the spices.

300 ml (10 fl oz) Greek strained
  yoghurt
¼ teaspoon cardamom seeds
Salt
15 g (½ oz) pistachio nuts

Put the yoghurt in a small bowl. Lightly roast the cardamom seeds in a dry frying-pan, crush lightly, then add to the yoghurt. Season with a little salt. Chop the pistachios finely. Serve the yoghurt in a small dish with the chopped pistachio nuts on the top.

Fresh Chutneys

Fresh Coriander and Chilli Chutney

This fresh chutney is extremely simple to make. It goes with a wide
variety of spiced dishes. Use it with barbecued vegetables too. The
chutney freezes well either in small pots or in ice-cube trays. Otherwise
keep it in the fridge for up to four days.

MAKES 350 ml (12 fl oz)

50 g (2 oz) fresh coriander
1 small fresh green chilli
50 g (2 oz) unsalted peanuts
Juice of 1½–2 lemons
Up to 6 tablespoons water

Put all the ingredients in a food processor or blender and blend until fairly smooth.

Fresh Tomato and Apple Chutney

Although this recipe doesn't contain any spices, it goes so well with
many of the ideas in this chapter, I decided to include it here. You can
spike the mixture with a little freshly grated ginger if you wish.

As you only need small quantities of this chutney, store it in an ice-cube
tray in the freezer. Defrost cubes when needed.

MAKES 475 ml (16 fl oz)

225 g (8 oz) tomatoes
1 eating apple, peeled and
    chopped
1 carrot, peeled and diced

Juice of ½ lemon
¼ teaspoon salt
¼ teaspoon sugar

Place the tomatoes in a large bowl and cover with boiling water. Leave for 3–4 minutes,
then drain well and remove the skins. Chop coarsely.

Put all the ingredients in a food processor or blender and process until smooth. Adjust
the seasoning. Serve at room temperature.

Hot Tomato and Apricot Chutney with Lime

Sweet, sharp and fiery, this fresh chutney is good with samosa, or *Minted Pilau with Peas and Pine Kernels* (see page 142).

MAKES 350–400 ml (12–14 fl oz)

225 g (8 oz) tomatoes
50 g (2 oz) dried apricots, finely
    chopped
1 fresh small green chilli
1 eating apple, peeled and
    chopped
1 carrot, peeled and diced
Juice of ½ lime
¼ teaspoon salt
¼ teaspoon sugar

Place the tomatoes in a large bowl and cover with boiling water. Leave for 3–4 minutes, then drain well and remove the skins. Chop coarsely.

Soak the apricots for 1 hour in hot water. Drain well.

Pre-heat the oven to 200°C/400°F/gas 6 and roast the green chilli for 10 minutes. Place in a polythene bag and leave to cool. Remove the skin and the seeds.

Put all the ingredients in a food processor or blender and process until smooth. Adjust the seasoning. Serve at room temperature.

PUDDINGS AND DESSERTS

On a day-to-day basis, I serve fresh fruit at the end of the meal. What a choice there is now. Gorgeous exotic salads of papaya, mango and passion fruit are hard to beat. Much less expensive but equally delicious are some of the traditional English apples, now widely on sale. Look out for the sweet Discovery and crisp Spartan, at their best for only a few months of the year. My children adore the buttery juiciness of pears, so I have become an expert at buying these to make sure we always have at least two ripe ones ready.

Dessert ideas like this, whilst they fit aptly into a book entitled fresh, hardly merit recipes and yet I felt this cookery book would not be complete without a chapter on sweet temptations to end a meal. Really the following puddings are just an indulgence, probably not to be eaten every day but enjoyed on special occasions. Some of them use new ingredients such as mascarpone cheese, the best pâtisserie chocolate, or filo pastry. I've also included a couple of my favourite traditional recipes such as plum crumble and sticky pudding.

Almond and Pecan Baklava

It is worth using unblanched almonds for this dish as their flavour when freshly skinned is marvellous. Unsalted pistachio can be hard to find. It is worth searching for them as they have a pretty colour and excellent taste. Otherwise, use more of the other nuts.

SERVES 6–8

100 g (4 oz) whole almonds
100 g (4 oz) pecans
100 g (4 oz) unsalted pistachios
75 g (3 oz) soft brown sugar
1 teaspoon cinnamon
½ teaspoon allspice
A grating of nutmeg

Zest of 1 lemon
100 g (4 oz) butter
12 sheets filo pastry (see page 47)
6 tablespoons honey
2 tablespoons water
2 tablespoons lemon juice

Pre-heat the oven to 200°C/400°F/gas 6.

Pour boiling water over the almonds and leave for 2 minutes, then remove the skins. Put the almonds and pecans on a baking tray and toast lightly for 4–5 minutes. Cool and then mix with the pistachios. Grind half the nuts very finely with the sugar, spices and lemon zest using a food processor or blender. Chop the remaining nuts quite finely by hand. Mix both lots of nuts together.

Melt the butter. Place a sheet of filo on a large baking sheet and brush well with butter. Put another sheet of filo on top and brush with butter, then repeat with a third sheet. Cover this with a third of the nut mixture. Then layer on another 3 sheets of filo brushing each with butter. Cover with another third of the nuts. Repeat these stages finishing off with the filo. Cut parallel lines down the filo sheets and then diagonal lines so that the sheets are cut into lozenges. Sprinkle with a little cold water to stop the edges curling up.

Bake for 20 minutes until the filo is quite brown, then lower the heat to 150°C/300°F/gas 2 for another 20 minutes so that the filo is well cooked.

Bring the honey and water to the boil for 1 minute, add the lemon juice and pour this over the cooked baklava. Leave to cool. Trim before serving.

Bilberry Brûlée

Bilberries, although they grow wild in some of the mountainous regions of this country, are not commercially cultivated. You can get myrtilles in jars or tins which are virtually the same thing. I like using them in this version of a classic recipe. The tart fruit works well with the rich custard. I also add yoghurt to give the dish more of a tang. Blackberries and blackcurrants, when in season, would also be fine for this recipe. You may wish to sweeten them.

MAKES 6–8 ramekins

225 g (8 oz) drained bilberries or
    myrtilles
4 egg yolks
25 g (1 oz) vanilla sugar
300 ml (10 fl oz) double cream

300 ml (10 fl oz) thick natural
    yoghurt
150 g (5 oz) golden granulated
    sugar
5 tablespoons water

Pre-heat the oven to 150°C/300°F/gas 2.

Lightly grease 6–8 ramekin dishes. Divide the bilberries between them. Sweeten if necessary.

Beat the egg yolks with the vanilla sugar. Heat the cream until virtually boiling then stir this into the egg yolk mixture adding the yoghurt. Divide this between the ramekin dishes. Place in a baking tray and pour boiling water round the ramekins up to the level of the custard. Bake for 30–35 minutes or until the custard has just set. Leave to chill for at least 2 hours. Overnight is fine.

For the caramelized topping, dissolve the golden granulated sugar in the water, then bring to the boil and boil vigorously for about 10 minutes. The mixture should darken slightly. Pour quickly over the ramekins and leave to set. Serve chilled.

Chocolate and Cinnamon Ice-cream

First, a word or two about chocolate. Do buy a good quality chocolate for cooking as you'll notice the difference. How do you tell quality? The easiest thing to look for is the percentage of cocoa solids used. This should be written on the package. The higher the percentage, the less room for padding, such as vegetable fat, which will dilute the flavour. True, it also means there is less room for sweetenings so the chocolate itself will taste bitter. It is easy though to adjust sweetening in any recipe.

Some of the other differences between brands of chocolate are more subtle. Rather like coffee, the selection of the cocoa beans, their drying and roasting will alter the flavour of the finished chocolate. The grinding of the ingredients, known as conching, is a vital part of the process. The finer the grinding and slower the mixing, the more the flavour will come through and the smoother the final texture will be. I have certainly tried chocolate with a high percentage of cocoa solids only to be disappointed by a powdery aftertaste. Finally, it is worth looking at what flavourings have been added. Proper vanilla extract is definitely the best.

Do store chocolate properly. This should be in a cool dry place at around 14–16°C/58–62°F.

Chocolate has an affinity with many other flavours, cinnamon is definitely one of them as this rich ice-cream shows. The cinnamon flavour is more pronounced the following day.

It is really best to use an ice-cream maker. There are some reasonably priced small machines. If you haven't one, then you must beat the mixture several times as it freezes to achieve a smooth texture.

SERVES 4

4 egg yolks
100 g (4 oz) light muscovado or soft brown sugar
300 ml (10 fl oz) milk

300 ml (10 fl oz) double cream
100 g (4 oz) dark cooking chocolate
½ teaspoon ground cinnamon

Beat the egg yolks and sugar together. Heat the milk to nearly boiling, then pour this over the egg yolks beating continuously. Put the saucepan on the heat and cook until the mixture begins to coat the back of the spoon. Leave to cool, then mix with the double cream.

Break the chocolate into pieces and melt it in a small bowl over a pan of hot water. Stir into the cream mixture and add the cinnamon. Using an ice-cream maker, churn and freeze for 20 minutes. Defrost a little before serving.

If you are making this ice-cream without an ice-cream maker, freeze the mixture, then after about 30 minutes remove from the freezer and beat thoroughly. Repeat this at least 4 times in order to get a smooth but light, finished texture. I don't think it is ever quite the same as ice-cream that is churned as it freezes, but the flavour is just as delicious.

Iced Mango Soufflé

I've missed making cold soufflés since becoming vegetarian as they do need gelatine and I've yet to find a vegetarian equivalent that works well. This recipe solves that problem as it is a semi-frozen mixture, lighter than ice-cream, which holds its shape enough to stand above the dish.

OVERLEAF
Left: *Iced Mango Soufflé*
Right: *Sticky Pudding* (page 182)

SERVES 4

3 eggs, separated
50 g (2 oz) caster sugar
2 tablespoons orange liqueur
2 teaspoons lemon juice

1 medium mango
15 g (½ oz) caster sugar or more
   to taste
150 ml (5 fl oz) whipping cream

Tie a collar made from baking parchment around a 600 ml (1 pint) soufflé dish. The collar should stand 5 cm (2 inch) above the rim of the dish.

Beat the egg yolks, then sieve them. Mix in the sugar, liqueur and lemon juice. Place the mixture in a small saucepan and cook over a very low heat – or in a double boiler – until it just thickens.

Peel the mango and remove the stone. Purée the flesh, adding sugar to taste. Measure out 150 ml (5 fl oz) of purée.

Mix the mango purée with the egg mixture. Then whip the cream until soft and fold in. Next whip the egg whites until stiff and fold in carefully.

Spoon the mixture into the prepared dish. Freeze for at least 2 hours. This should give time for the outside to freeze solid so that you can remove the paper collar. The middle will have a soft consistency.

Lime and Passion Fruit Pavlova

Pavlova is like a meringue but sticky inside. It is quite hard to tell when it is cooked. If you are unsure, I think it is best to leave it undisturbed in a cool oven rather than try to do anything awkward such as turn the meringue over – this usually has disastrous consequences. I like a simple topping for pavlova.

Passion fruit are rather dull-looking, small, wrinkly specimens quite concealing their inner delights. They contain hundreds of edible black seeds, sweet, sharp and crunchy all at the same time and the pulp, such as there is, is a golden colour and pleasantly perfumed.

SERVES 4

3 egg whites
A pinch of salt
¼ teaspoon cream of tartar
175 g (6 oz) golden caster sugar
3 teaspoons cornflour

1½ teaspoons white wine vinegar
4 passion fruit
Zest of 1 lime
300 ml (10 fl oz) double cream

Pre-heat the oven to 140°C/275°F/gas 1.

Beat the egg whites with the salt and cream of tartar until stiff. Add the sugar a teaspoon at a time, whisking in well. Then beat in the cornflour and vinegar.

Mark a circle 20 cm (8 inches) in diameter on a sheet of baking parchment. Pile the egg white mixture onto it. Make an indentation in the centre. Bake for 2 hours and leave to cool completely.

For the topping, halve the passion fruit and scoop out the seeds and pulp. Mix with the lime zest. Whip the double cream and then fold in the passion fruit mixture. Spoon the cream over the pavlova base. Leave for an hour or so before serving.

Melon and Strawberry Brochettes with Sabayon Sauce

Shops now stock a wonderful variety of melons with distinctive flavours and colours ranging from pale yellow to rich pink. When buying melon, look for those that seem heavy for their size. Smell them too. I find the riper ones smell sweet and sometimes scented. Watch out for bruises and soft patches on the skin, though ripe melons can be soft at the stalk end.

Cantaloupe: round, heavily textured skin. Comes in various sizes, orange flesh.

Charantais: delicious, perfumed orange flesh, green skin.

Galia: round, slightly larger than the Ogen. Crinkly skin. Green flesh. Sweet flavour.

Honeydew: yellow skin when ripe. Pale yellow almost white flesh. Can be delicious or very disappointing.

Ogen: green flesh, sweet and juicy. One of the smallest melons.

Piel de Sapo: distinctive mottled skin like a toad as the name implies. Ripe specimens can be very sweet almost sugary.

A mixture of coloured melons makes a most effective fruit skewer. Buy bamboo satay skewers which are quite short. Add a strawberry or two for a splash of colour and serve with a creamy alcoholic sauce.

SERVES 6–8

For the sauce

3 egg yolks
1 egg
75 g (3 oz) caster sugar
150 ml (5 fl oz) sweet wine wine

For the brochettes

3 contrasting melons
50–75 g (2–3 oz) strawberries

Whisk the egg yolks and whole egg with the sugar in a saucepan over a medium heat, until pale and foaming. Stand the pan in another pan containing about 2.5 cm (1 inch) boiling water. Pour the wine into the egg mixture, beating all the time. Keep beating the mixture until it is thick enough to coat the back of a spoon. Then transfer the sauce to a bowl standing in a larger bowl of ice-cubes and whisk for about 4 minutes until the sauce is cool.

Using a melon baller, make equal quantities of balls from different coloured melons. Alternatively, cut them into equal-sized cubes. Thread the melon pieces onto skewers along with the strawberries. Serve 2 or 3 skewers per person depending on the size of the skewer. Spoon 2–3 tablespoons of the sauce on a shallow plate for each person and lay the fruit skewers in the sauce. Serve chilled.

Orange Cheese with Passion Fruit and Orange Sauce

Hung cheeses such as this are worth the trouble. The excess liquid gradually drips away leaving you with a mousse-like cream which is lightly set. This process avoids the need for gelatine, which is not vegetarian, or substitutes which I don't find work at all well. This type of cheese can be flavoured in many ways, for example with sweet spices or dried fruits. I like the sharpness of citrus fruit. The clean taste goes well with the distinctive perfumed flavour of passion fruit.

SERVES 4

For the cheese

225 g (8 oz) cream cheese
2 tablespoons white caster sugar
Zest of 1 large orange
2 cloves, ground
2 large egg whites

For the sauce

3 passion fruit
150 ml (5 fl oz) fresh orange juice
*   plus 1 tablespoon*
3 tablespoons caster sugar
1 teaspoon arrowroot

2 oranges

Beat the cream cheese with the sugar, orange zest and cloves. Then whisk the egg whites until stiff and fold in. Spoon the mixture into a piece of muslin and leave hanging in a cool place for at least 4 hours or overnight. Spoon into ramekins lined with greaseproof paper and chill.

To make the sauce, scoop out the passion fruit seeds and pulp. Mix with 150 ml (5 fl oz) orange juice and sugar. Bring to the boil and simmer for 5 minutes then strain. Dissolve the arrowroot in the remaining 1 tablespoon orange juice. Mix into the sauce and simmer for 5 minutes, stirring well. Leave to cool.

Peel and segment the oranges. Chill well.

To serve, turn out the cheese onto individual plates and arrange the orange segments to one side of them. Pour the sauce over the segments.

Pear and Almond Tart

A rich yet light tart ideal as a pudding or with afternoon tea.

SERVES 4–6

For the pastry

175 g (6 oz) plain white flour
A pinch of salt
75 g (3 oz) butter

1 tablespoon light muscovado sugar
1 egg, beaten
1 egg yolk

For the filling

100 g (4 oz) butter
100 g (4 oz) light muscovado sugar
2 eggs

50 g (2 oz) self-raising flour
100 g (4 oz) ground almonds
1 tablespoon brandy
1 large ripe pear

First make the pastry. Mix the flour and salt in a bowl and rub in the butter until the mixture resembles fine breadcrumbs. Mix in the sugar. Add the egg and egg yolk and draw the mixture together to make a soft dough. Leave to rest for 10–15 minutes. Roll out thinly and line a 20 cm (8 inch) deep flan dish.

To make the filling. Beat the butter with the sugar until the mixture is light and fluffy. Add the eggs one at a time (if the mixture looks as though it will curdle add a little flour). Beat in the flour and ground almonds, then add the brandy.

Pre-heat the oven to 200°c/400°F/gas 6.

Peel the pear and divide into 8. Arrange the pieces around the pastry. Cover with the almond filling. Bake for 35 minutes or until the filling has set. Serve warm or at room temperature.

Plum Crumble with Hazelnut Topping

Plums vary considerably in flavour. The job of selecting them is made more difficult by the fact that they are often still unripe when in the shop, so you can't taste them first. On the whole I've found the golden and green-skinned varieties are sweeter to taste, yet occasionally I've managed to buy some delicious plums with an almost blue skin.

SERVES 4

450 g (1 lb) ripe plums
50 g (2 oz) large seedless raisins
(preferably Lexia)
2 tablespoons clear honey

For the topping

100 g (4 oz) hazelnuts
100 g (4 oz) plain flour
50 g (2 oz) sugar
50 g (2 oz) butter

Pre-heat the oven to 200°C/400°F/gas 6.

Stew the plums and raisins with the honey for about 10 minutes or until the plums are soft. Cool and remove the stones.

For the topping, toast the hazelnuts on a baking sheet in the oven for 6 minutes. Cool and remove the skins by rubbing several nuts at a time between your hands. Chop the nuts roughly.

Mix the flour and sugar together, then rub in the butter. Stir in the nuts.

Put the fruit mixture in an ovenproof bowl, cover with topping. Bake at 190°C/375°F/gas 5 for about 20–25 minutes. Serve hot or warm.

Rhubarb Soufflé

Poor old rhubarb! Watery, tough chunks of this stalk served with an imitation custard have not enhanced its reputation. I have tasted some delicious rhubarb compote sold in jars which can be eaten as it is or quickly mixed with cream or crème fraîche for a fool. Rhubarb is easy to cook and there is little waste. The trick is to avoid anything old as it will be tough. Look for young pink skins rather than anything green.

This is like a feather-light version of rhubarb and custard but comes hot.

SERVES 6

450 g (1 lb) rhubarb
100 g (4 oz) white caster sugar
  plus extra for sprinkling
Zest of ½ lemon

½ teaspoon ground ginger
4 eggs, separated
300 ml (10 fl oz) double cream,
  whipped

You'll need 6 × 200 ml (7 fl oz) soufflé dishes or large ramekins. Grease the dishes and sprinkle with a little caster sugar.

Trim the rhubarb, place in a pan with the 100 g (4 oz) sugar, lemon zest and ginger and cook. Add the egg yolks while the mixture is still warm. Beat in well and leave to cool. Fold in the whipped cream.

Then beat the egg whites until stiff and fold in.

Pre-heat the oven to 190°C/375°F/gas 5. Divide the mixture between the prepared dishes and place them in a large ovenproof dish. Fill the dish with boiling water to reach about half-way up the ramekin dishes. Bake for 20 minutes or until well risen and just firm to the touch. Serve immediately.

Spiced Apple Pancakes with Calvados Sauce

I use eating apples for this pudding as they keep some texture once cooked. A crisp Discovery or Royal Gala have a good flavour.

SERVES 4

For the pancakes

300 ml (10 fl oz) milk
1 egg
1 teaspoon oil
125 g (4 oz) wholemeal flour

Pinch salt
1 tablespoon soft brown
  sugar
A little oil for frying

For the filling

25 g (1 oz) butter
450 g (1 lb) eating apples
  (weighed when peeled,
  cored and
  chopped)
50 g (2 oz) raisins

50 g (2 oz) pecan nuts, coarsely
  chopped
25 g (1 oz) muscovado sugar
Zest of 1 lemon
½ teaspoon allspice
A grating of nutmeg

For the sauce

3 tablespoons Calvados
50 g (2 oz) unsalted butter

25 g (1 oz) muscovado sugar
Juice of 1 lemon

Whipped cream to serve

Using a food processor or blender, mix the milk, egg and oil together for 30 seconds. Then add the flour, salt and sugar and blend again until smooth. Leave to stand for 20 minutes.

Using a small, preferably non stick pan, heat a little oil and when the pan is smoking, add 1½ tablespoons of batter and fry the pancake for 2–3 minutes on each side.

Once made, keep the pancakes warm wrapped in foil in a low oven. To make the filling, melt the butter and add the chopped apples, raisins, nuts and sugar. Cover the mixture with a piece of buttered paper then a lid. Cook for about 10 minutes or until the apple is soft. Add the lemon zest and spices. Sweeten a little more if necessary. Keep warm.

For the sauce, heat the Calvados over a gentle heat, light it and let it burn until the flames die down. In a separate pan, melt the butter then stir in the Calvados, sugar and lemon juice. Heat gently until the sugar dissolves.

Fill each pancake with 2 tablespoons of apple mixture, roll up and drizzle over the warm sauce. Serve with whipped cream.

Sticky Pudding

Crème fraîche adds a light tang to this rich pudding.

SERVES 4

For the topping

50 g (2 oz) butter
100 g (4 oz) dark muscovado sugar

3 tablespoons crème fraîche
2 tablespoons fresh orange juice

For the pudding

100 g (4 oz) butter
100 g (4 oz) soft brown sugar
2 eggs
100 g (4 oz) crème fraîche
100 g (4 oz) self-raising wholemeal flour

1 teaspoon baking powder
225 (8 oz) grated carrot
50 g (2 oz) chopped walnuts
50 g (2 oz) sultanas
Rind of 1 orange

For the topping, heat the butter and sugar, boil for 3 minutes, stir in the crème fraîche and orange juice.

For the pudding, cream the butter and sugar then beat in the eggs and the crème fraîche. Fold in the flour and baking powder, then quickly mix in the remaining ingredients. Grease 2 × 900 ml (1½ pints) pudding basins. Pour 2 tablespoons of topping into each greased pudding dish and divide the pudding mixture between them. Cover the basins with a double layer of greaseproof paper and foil and tie securely with string. It is easier to undo a bow than a knot. Put the puddings into a large pan of boiling water. Steam for 1½–1¾ hours. Check occasionally on the water content. Turn out and serve hot with the remaining sauce.

Vanilla Pears with Caramel Sauce

I love the flavour of pear with vanilla. The purée is thickened with mascarpone cheese and a custard and served with a wickedly sweet sauce. Be careful when buying vanilla extract. Anything with the words 'flavoured' or 'flavouring' on the label is likely to be synthetic, and the flavour is just not so good. Vanilla extract itself is delicious but powerful so do add it cautiously.

MAKES 4 generous or 6 smaller portions

For the purée

4 pears
2 tablespoons caster sugar

50 ml (2 fl oz) water
100 g (4 oz) mascarpone cheese

For the custard

1 egg
25 g (1 oz) sugar

150 ml (5 fl oz) milk
A few drops of vanilla extract

For the sauce

100 g (4 oz) granulated sugar
150 ml (5 fl oz) water or
     reserved pear juice

25 g (1 oz) butter
3 tablespoons single cream

Peel the pears and chop roughly. Dissolve the sugar in the water add the pears and stew until soft. Leave to cool, drain (reserving the juice), then purée with the mascarpone.

To make the custard, whisk the egg with the sugar. Warm the milk in a saucepan, then whisk into the egg mix. Add the vanilla extract. Return the pan to the heat and cook until the mixture thickens, stirring frequently. Leave to cool then blend into the pear mixture. Chill.

For the sauce, put the sugar and water, or reserved pear juice, in a heavy pan. Stir over a gentle heat until the sugar has dissolved. Bring to a fast boil and boil to a caramel (174°C/345°F on a sugar thermometer) for 5 minutes. Leave to cool slightly then whisk in the butter. Then whisk in the cream. Leave to cool.

Divide the pear purée into tall glasses and top with a portion of sauce (there may be some left over). Chill again.

SPECIAL BREADS

Freshly baked bread! I don't think there is anything that quite beats it. We are great bread eaters in our house, so much so that the poor local ducks never get so much as a look-in. There's rarely a stale crust.

I love bread-making, finding it one of the most satisfying processes in cooking. For standard fare I bake wholemeal loaves, but I am increasingly making a range of ethnic and continental breads to serve with food. I don't feel that these are an 'add on' or something to mop up a few juices, they are an integral and sophisticated part of a meal.

I like to make my own breads as I feel I've got more flexibility and control over ingredients. If you haven't time for home baking, I think you'll find the bread sections of supermarkets are one of the most interesting to raid.

I've started this chapter with a basic recipe as I think it helps to be well practised with simple dough. The more you make the easier it is to have a feel for when the dough is right, when it has risen enough and when it is cooked. Once you are confident with the look and feel of basic bread, it's easy to start adding extra ingredients such as oil, nuts, yoghurt and so on, all of which will change the texture and nature of the dough.

Just a word or two about the principal ingredients, flour and yeast.

Flour

Any plain flour (white, brown, unbleached, organic or whatever) will make bread, but I think it is worth investing in different types of flours as they will subtly alter the end result.

I have three basic flours for bread-making (organic if I can get it); strong stone-ground wholemeal, strong unbleached white, and plain unbleached white. For basic loaves, brown or white, I use strong flour. Strong flour is made from hard wheat which contains more gluten, absorbs more water and will rise well. Soft wheat, milled to make plain flour which is generally used in cakes and pastries, is not so springy and seems to work better with the more cake-like breads (i.e. those where you are adding a higher proportion of fats such as olive oil).

184

Yeast

I make all my bread with easy-blend yeast. It is exactly as it says, easy-blend, and also easy to buy and keep in stock. I do miss the smell of fresh yeast and its magic first stir-rings, but I can't buy it locally. The results with easy-blend yeast are just as good and over the years I have only had two sachets go flat on me.

Basic Bread

The recipe I've given here is for the batter method of making bread which is different from the traditional method, but I think produces good results. The batter method is as it sounds. The first stage is to make a batter using all the water and yeast and adding enough flour until the mixture is the texture of pancake batter. You can then leave this for up to an hour before adding the remaining ingredients. Once you have made a dough, you can simply knead it and put it straight in tins to bake. Otherwise knead it, then let it rise then knock back. Do this by punching the risen dough firmly and knead again. A second rise can give the bread a better flavour and consistency.

I've given quantities for using a whole bag of flour as this saves any weighing out. Make half quantities if you prefer.

MAKES 2 large loaves

2 sachets easy-blend yeast
900 ml (1½ pints) warm water
1.5 kg (3¼ lb) strong wholemeal
    bread flour
3 teaspoons salt
2 tablespoons olive oil

Mix the yeast and the water together. Stir in about a quarter of the flour, mixing with a wooden spoon, until the batter is roughly the consistency of a pancake batter. Cover with cling film and leave for up to an hour. Add the salt to the remaining flour then add this with the oil to the batter. At first beat it in with a spoon and then, as the dough becomes thicker, mix with your hands to make a dough. Add more warm water if necessary. Knead well.

Leave to rise again in a clean bowl covered with cling film or divide in two and shape each piece to fit an oiled 900 g (2 lb) loaf tin. Leave to prove until doubled in size. Pre-heat the oven to 220°C/425°F/gas 7. Then bake the loaves for 35–40 minutes or until the loaf sounds hollow when tapped on the base. Leave to cool on a wire rack. If you put the dough to rise in the bowl, leave until the dough has doubled in size then knock back, divide and prepare the dough for the tins. Bake as above.

Brioche

Brioche dough is rich and buttery. It needs to be beaten very thoroughly and given plenty of time to chill or it is simply too sticky to manage. Whether you are making buns or pastry, the dough must be made the day before, then left in the fridge overnight. This does mean the main effort is out of the way, and the following day it is very quick to roll out or shape. Brioche buns can be served plain or filled with salads. Rolled out, the dough makes an excellent pastry for special occasions.

MAKES 6 individual brioche buns

225 g (8 oz) unbleached white flour	*3 tablespoons milk at room temperature*
1 teaspoon sugar	*2 eggs, beaten*
1 sachet easy-blend yeast	*100 g (4 oz) butter, softened*
1 teaspoon salt	*1 egg yolk*
	A pinch of salt

Put the flour, sugar, yeast and 1 teaspoon salt into a bowl and mix together. Make a well in the centre, pour in the milk and whole eggs. Beat well until evenly combined. Beat in the softened butter a little piece at a time. Beat well in between each addition to give a smooth glossy dough. Add a little more flour if the dough is too slack. Put the dough in a clean bowl, cover with cling film and leave to rise for 1½ hours. Knock back and return to the bowl, cover with cling film and leave overnight in the fridge.

For individual brioche buns, divide into 6 portions. Form into balls and put in greased deep muffin tins. Leave to prove until doubled in size (this can take 2–3 hours if the dough is very cold). Beat the egg yolk and salt together and use some to brush over the dough. Pre-heat the oven to 220°C/425°F/gas 7 and bake for 10 minutes. Then remove from oven and glaze again. Return to the oven for a further 5 minutes. Remove from tin and cool on a wire rack.

Cheese and Caraway Scones

Adding potato to a scone mixture seems to make them lighter and crisper rather than the reverse. I like making miniature versions of these to serve with a first course or light lunch dish, and larger ones as a substitute for sandwiches.

MAKES 8–12

100 g (4 oz) potato, peeled and diced
225 g (8 oz) self-raising wholemeal flour
¼ teaspoon salt
40 g (1½ oz) butter

75 g (3 oz) Cheddar cheese, grated
1½ teaspoons caraway seeds
150 ml (5 fl oz) milk plus a little extra
Freshly grated Parmesan for sprinkling

Cook the potato in boiling water until soft. Drain and then mash until smooth. Leave to cool.

Mix the flour and salt in a bowl. Rub in the potato, then rub in the butter and mix in the cheese and caraway seeds.

Pour in the milk and quickly mix to a dough with a knife. Knead lightly. On a floured board, roll out thickly and cut into rounds. Pre-heat the oven to 200°C/400°F/gas 6. Place the scones on a greased baking sheet and brush with a little milk and sprinkle over some grated Parmesan. Bake for 15–18 minutes or until cooked. Leave to cool on a wire rack.

Cheese and Sesame Focaccia

Focaccia are baked in large rounds dotted with holes which gives the bread a distinctive appearance once cooked. The dough is made with plenty of olive oil which gives it a delicious flavour. Bake it plain or add a cheese and sesame topping as in this version. Focaccia is best eaten very fresh. If you have some left over use it for Bruschetta (see page 200).

Once baked focaccia can be filled with a light, leafy salad or some of the more substantial fillings on pages 195–7.

MAKES 2 large rounds

1 sachet easy-blend yeast
450 ml (15 fl oz) warm water
750 g (1½ lb) plain white flour
1½ teaspoons salt
65 ml (2½ fl oz) olive oil
2 tablespoons olive oil for
brushing

1–2 tablespoons sesame
seeds
Salt for sprinkling
50 g (2 oz) fresh Parmesan or
pecorino, grated
Freshly ground black pepper

Mix the yeast with the water and about a quarter of the flour. Stir to make a batter and leave for 10–15 minutes in a warm place. Add the remaining flour, salt and 65 ml (2½ fl oz) olive oil. Knead for 5 minutes or until smooth, then put in a clean bowl, cover with cling film and leave to rise. Knock back and form into 2 large rounds and place on an oiled baking sheet. Prove for 15 minutes.

Pre-heat the oven to 200°C/400°F/gas 6. Make holes over the surface of the dough using the end of a wooden spoon dipped in flour. Brush each round with olive oil and sprinkle over with sesame seeds and extra salt. Bake for 15 minutes. Sprinkle over the cheese and black pepper and bake for a further 5 minutes. Cool on a wire rack.

Enriched White Plait
with Egg Glaze

An egg yolk glaze gives this loaf a shiny golden crust. The inside is soft and white. I especially like this sort of bread at tea time as it is excellent with jam.

A plait is very easy to make. Once you have rolled out the three ropes of dough, lay them side by side and begin plaiting in the middle as this will help you get an evenly sized plait rather than one which is thin at one end and thick at the other.

MAKES 1 plait

250 ml (8 fl oz) tepid milk
1 sachet easy-blend yeast
450 g (1 lb) strong white flour
1 teaspoon salt

1 egg (at room temperature),
beaten
1 egg yolk
A pinch of salt

Make a batter by beating together the milk, yeast and a quarter of the flour. Leave for 15 minutes.

Mix in the remaining flour, 1 teaspoon salt, and beaten egg. Draw the ingredients together to make a dough, then knead for 10 minutes. Put in a clean bowl, cover with cling film and leave for 1 hour at room temperature.

Knock back and divide the dough into 3. Roll into equal length ropes. Then plait them from the centre towards one end, then turn the dough round and plait towards the other end. Place on a greased baking sheet and leave to prove, covered with a clean cloth, for 20–30 minutes.

Pre-heat the oven to 220°C/425°F/gas 7. Bake the plait for 10 minutes. Beat the egg yolk with the pinch of salt and brush the loaf with it. Return the loaf to the oven for a further 10 minutes or until the loaf is cooked. Cool on a wire rack.

Garlic and Coriander Nan

These delicious breads have a distinctive chewy texture. I like adding coriander and garlic, though you can make plain versions. Wholemeal nan do not puff up as much as those made with white flour. Serve nan with spiced dishes such as *Pumpkin Korma* (page 165), or *Spiced Okra and Potato* (page 59).

MAKES 10 medium rounds

450 g (1 lb) plain wholemeal or white flour
1 teaspoon baking powder
¼ teaspoon salt
4 tablespoons chopped fresh coriander

6 cloves garlic, peeled and chopped
300–350 ml (10–12 fl oz) natural yoghurt
Melted butter to serve

Mix together the flour, baking powder, salt, coriander and garlic. Stir in enough yoghurt to make a soft dough. Knead until smooth. Heat a dry heavy-based frying-pan on a high heat until very hot.

Divide the dough into 10 equal portions. Roll each portion into a round about 10 cm (4 inches) in diameter on a lightly floured surface.

Fry each round until puffed up like a balloon, turn over and fry for a few minutes more. Pile up the cooked nan under a cloth. Serve warm brushed with melted butter.

Oaten Rolls

Porridge oat flakes added to a bread dough give a good chewy texture and creamy flavour. However, they also make the dough softer and stickier than an ordinary dough. Don't be tempted to add too much extra flour or the resulting bread will be hard.

MAKES 12 rolls

100 g (4 oz) porridge oats
375–425 ml (13–15 fl oz) warm
    water
1 sachet easy-blend yeast

450 g (1 lb) plain white flour
1 teaspoon salt
1 tablespoon olive oil

Using a large bowl, soak the oats in the water and mix in the yeast. Leave for 1 hour.

Stir in the flour, salt and oil and work to a soft dough. Put in a clean bowl covered with cling film and leave to rest for 1 hour. Knock back, dusting the surface with a little flour if necessary, and divide into 12 equal pieces. Shape each one into a roll and place on a greased baking sheet. Leave to rise for 30 minutes.

Pre-heat the oven to 220°C/425°F/gas 7 and bake the rolls for 15–20 minutes. Cool on a wire rack.

Olive and Walnut Ring

Baking bread in a ring makes a good centrepiece for a buffet or a picnic.
Either fill the bread itself or put a dip or spread in a bowl and
wedge it in the middle.

MAKES 1 ring

1 sachet easy-blend yeast
450 ml (15 fl oz) warm water
750 g (1½ lb) plain white flour
1½ teaspoons salt
2 tablespoons walnut oil

50 g (2 oz) pitted black olives,
    coarsely chopped
50 g (2 oz) shelled walnuts,
    coarsely chopped

Mix the yeast with the water and about a quarter of the flour. Stir to make a batter and leave for 10–15 minutes in a warm place. Then add the remaining flour, salt and walnut oil. Knead for 10 minutes put in a clean bowl covered with cling film, then leave to rise for 1–1½ hours. Knock back and roll out into an oblong about 20 × 25 cm (8 × 10 in).

Arrange the pieces of olives and walnuts over the top and roll up the dough starting at one of the long edges. Shape the roll into a ring, place on a greased baking sheet. Using scissors snip the ring at intervals of about 6 cm (2 in) all the way round. Prove for 15 minutes. Pre-heat the oven to 200°C/400°F/gas 6 and bake the ring for 30 minutes. Cool on a wire rack.

PREVIOUS PAGES
Cheese and Seame Focaccia (page 187) with *Sun-dried Tomato Bread* (page 195) with
Roasted Aubergine, Mozzarella, Sun-dried Tomato and Basil filling (page 197)

Pizza Dough with Olive Oil

MAKES 1 round

1 sachet easy-blend yeast
1 teaspoon sugar
200 ml (7 fl oz) warm water

350 g (12 oz) plain white or wholemeal flour
1 teaspoon salt
1–2 tablespoons olive oil

To make the base, mix the yeast with the sugar and warm water. Add about a quarter of the flour and beat well to a smooth batter. Leave for 10 minutes.

Mix the salt with the remaining flour. Mix into the batter, add the olive oil and knead well to make a smooth dough. Add more flour if necessary. Pre-heat the oven to 200°C/400°F/gas 6. Roll out either in a round or oblong. Prick with a fork. With wholemeal dough, bake for 5 minutes before adding the topping. With a white dough simply spread on the topping.

Seeded Baguette

Linseed and sesame seeds work very well in bread, adding both a pleasant crunchy texture and nutty flavour. Baguettes are a useful shape to present whole, small or large. Fill them for picnics or slice diagonally and serve with soup.

MAKES 2 baguettes

750 g (1½ lb) strong white flour
1½ teaspoons salt
1 sachet easy-blend yeast
40 g (1½ oz) linseed

40 g (1½ oz) sesame seeds
450 ml (15 fl oz) warm water
1 tablespoon sunflower oil

Mix together the flour, salt, yeast and seeds in a large bowl. Pour on the warm water and oil and make a soft dough. Knead well for several minutes. Put in a clean bowl, cover with cling film and leave to rise for an hour or so.

Knock back and knead again. Divide in two. Shape each half of the dough into a baguette shape and place on an oiled sheet. Leave to rise for 40 minutes or until doubled in size. Pre-heat the oven to 220°C/425°F/gas 7 and bake the baguettes for 25 minutes. Cool on a wire rack.

Seeded Cornbread

This version of golden cornbread has a buttery flavour and cake-like texture. It makes a quick accompaniment to a casserole dish, or can be eaten with salads.

SERVES 6–8

100 g (4 oz) plain wholemeal flour
100 g (4 oz) maize meal or cornmeal
50 g (2 oz) golden caster sugar
2½ teaspoons baking powder
½ teaspoon salt
1 tablespoon sesame seeds
2 eggs
250 ml (8 fl oz) milk
50 g (2 oz) butter

Pre-heat the oven to 200°C/400°F/gas 6. Mix both the flours, sugar, baking powder, salt and sesame seeds together. Beat the eggs with the milk. Melt the butter and whisk into the milk and egg mixture. Add this liquid to the dry ingredients and mix quickly. Pour into a greased ovenproof 20 × 20 cm (8 × 8 in) dish and bake for 20 minutes. Serve hot in wedges.

Spiced Poori

Poori make a good appetizer to serve with dips. They are at their crispest when just made so try to leave preparing them until the last minute. If prepared in advance they are just as tasty but will be softer and not so puffed up.

To make successful poori, it is important to get the oil hot and the poori thin and even.

MAKES 20–25

225 g (8 oz) plain white flour
¼ teaspoon asafoetida (page 59)
¼ teaspoon turmeric
¼ teaspoon chilli powder
¼ teaspoon salt
2 tablespoons oil
9 tablespoons warm water
Oil for rubbing into the rolling board
Oil for deep-frying

Mix the flour with the spices and salt and work in the 2 tablespoons oil. Make a well in the centre, then add most of the warm water. Mix well and add a little more water if necessary to make a soft dough. Knead briefly.

Divide the dough into walnut-sized lumps weighing about 15 g (½ oz). Roll each into a ball in your hands then press into a small thick circle.

Rub some oil into a bread board, then roll out each circle of dough to a thin circle about 6 cm (2½ inches) in diameter.

Heat about 5 cm (2 in) depth of oil in a wide saucepan or small deep frying-pan. When the oil is really hot, slide in 1 or 2 poori at a time. Press under the surface of the oil with a slotted spoon. They should expand as they cook. Turn them over, cook briefly, then remove from the pan and drain on kitchen paper.

Sun-dried Tomato Bread

I like to put large pieces of sun-dried tomatoes into dough as I find small pieces just get lost. If the larger pieces fall out as you knead, simply push them back in.

MAKES 1 loaf

1 sachet easy-blend yeast
450 ml (15 fl oz) warm water
750 g (1½ lb) plain white flour
1½ teaspoons salt
65 ml (2½ fl oz) olive oil

12 sun-dried tomatoes (in oil),
*   sliced lengthwise*
1 tablespoon olive oil
½ teaspoon coarse sea salt

Mix the yeast with the water and about a quarter of the flour. Stir to make a batter and leave for 10–15 minutes in a warm place. Add the remaining flour, salt and olive oil. Knead for 10 minutes, put in a clean bowl covered with cling film and then leave to rise for 1–1½ hours.

Knock back and flatten the dough. Lay on the tomatoes and roll it up. Form into a large round and place on a baking sheet. Prove for 15 minutes.

Pre-heat the oven to 200°C/400°F/gas 6. Make holes over the surface of the dough using the end of a wooden spoon dipped in flour. Brush with 1 tablespoon olive oil and sprinkle with the coarse sea salt. Bake for 30 minutes. Cool on a wire rack.

Fillings for Breads and Sandwiches

I like the sort of sandwiches that you need both hands to tackle. Not very elegant, true, but there is something special about having a fresh and tasty meal at your finger-tips.

Here are a few recipes for fillings which can be matched with a variety of breads, home-made or shop-bought. For other ideas on fillings, you can also use many of the salads in the chapter on salad leaves, as well as some of the salads and marinades in the chapter on oils.

Cream Cheese and Dill Spread
with Gherkins

MAKES 150–175 g (5–6 oz)

100 g (4 oz) cream cheese
2–3 tablespoons chopped fresh dill
1 spring onion, diced

1 teaspoon cider vinegar
Salt and freshly ground black pepper
4 cocktail gherkins

Mix the cream cheese with the dill, spring onion and cider vinegar. Season to taste.

Split the bread of your choice and butter if you wish. Spread thickly with the cream cheese spread. Add some sliced gherkins.

Feta Cheese with Radish
and Spring Onion

Feta cheese with its salty flavour is ideal with bread. I've combined it here with olive oil and yoghurt to make a creamy dressing.

MAKES 200–250 g (7–8 oz)

For the dressing

6 tablespoons olive oil
1 tablespoon white wine vinegar
50 g (2 oz) feta cheese
4 tablespoons Greek yoghurt

2 teaspoons chopped fresh oregano
1 teaspoon chopped fresh thyme
Salt and freshly ground black pepper

For the salad filling

175 g (6 oz) radishes
4 spring onions
Cos or Little Gem lettuce
Extra olive oil

Place the olive oil, wine vinegar, feta, yoghurt and herbs in a food processor or blender and process until smooth. Adjust the seasoning.

For the salad filling, slice the radishes and chop the spring onions. Wash and dry the lettuce. Split the bread of your choice, brush with oil, put in a few lettuce leaves, then add the salad ingredients and coat liberally with the dressing.

Guacamole with Roasted Corn and Peppers

You could use taco shells instead of bread with this filling.

FILLS 4–6 tacos

For the guacamole

1 clove garlic, peeled
A pinch of salt
1 avocado, peeled and stone
    removed

1 tablespoon lemon juice
1 tablespoon olive oil
Freshly ground black
    pepper

1 red pepper
1 tablespoon sunflower oil
75 g (3 oz) baby sweetcorn

Salt and freshly ground black
    pepper
Little Gem lettuce, shredded

For the guacamole, put the garlic and salt in a blender and process. Then add the avocado, lemon juice and olive oil and process until smooth. Season to taste.

Pre-heat the oven to 200°C/400°F/gas 6. Rub the pepper with a little of the oil and bake for 30–40 minutes or until the skin is charred. Cool, then peel and remove the seeds. Cut the pepper in thin slices. Toss the baby sweetcorn in the remaining oil and season. Bake on a sheet of parchment for 15 minutes.

Fill your chosen bread with shredded lettuce, roast baby corn, slices of pepper, and a portion of guacamole.

Roasted Aubergine, Mozzarella, Sun-dried Tomato and Basil

1 aubergine
1 tablespoon olive oil
Salt and freshly ground black
    pepper
Extra olive oil

100 g (4 oz) mozzarella
4–6 sun-dried tomatoes (in oil),
    cut in strips
8 basil leaves

Pre-heat the oven to 200°C/400°F/gas 6. Slice the aubergine thickly and brush with oil. Season well. Bake the slices on a baking sheet for 15–20 minutes or until soft. Leave to cool.

To fill your chosen bread, brush the inside with olive oil and layer in slices of aubergine, mozzarella, sun-dried tomato strips and basil leaves. Add extra seasoning to taste.

SUMMER FARE

MEZZE

Artichoke Heart Salad
Broccoli and Parmesan Roulade
with Red Pepper Cream
Bruschetta
Croûtons and Crudités
with Almond Mayonnaise
Ratatouille Vinaigrette
Roquefort and Rice
with Roasted Walnuts

I love the idea of a mezze, a Middle Eastern word really implying hors-d'œuvres. I see it in terms of a buffet comprising numerous small dishes. The choice needn't be confined to so-called starters or main courses, some dishes can be hot, some cold. It is simply an array of different foods from which to make a meal. I find this fluid style of eating very appealing and very suitable for many of the recipes I've given in this book. If one idea doesn't quite make a meal, put

two or three things together, add a special bread, a simple dip and a bowl of olives and you have a leisurely feast.

Here are some ideas for a mezze but there are other recipes in this book that are suitable too such as *Baked Italian Tomatoes with Basil and Balsamic Vinegar* (page 93), *Roasted Baby Sweetcorn with Rosemary* (page 20), *Marinated Mushrooms with Lemon and Green Peppercorns* (page 84) and *Marinated Feta with Sun-dried Tomatoes* (page 78).

Artichoke Heart Salad

SERVES 4

For the dressing

5 tablespoons olive oil
2 tablespoons red wine vinegar
1 tablespoon black olive paste or
    8–10 finely chopped olives
1 clove garlic, peeled and crushed

1 teaspoon chopped fresh thyme
½ teaspoon brown sugar
Salt and freshly ground black
    pepper

For the salad

8 artichoke hearts in oil
1 Italian beef tomato
50–75 g (2–3 oz) mixed salad
    leaves (such as endive, rocket)
3 spring onions, diced

Prepare the dressing by mixing all the ingredients together. Season to taste.

For the salad, halve the artichoke hearts and slice the tomato thickly.

Line a bowl with salad leaves, lay the artichokes, tomato slices and spring onions on top and drizzle over the dressing. There may be a little dressing left over. Serve immediately.

Broccoli and Parmesan Roulade with Red Pepper Cream

A roulade is like a flat soufflé, baked and then rolled up. Served cold in slices, it is good as part of a light summer meal. I've filled this roulade with a colourful, full-flavoured red pepper purée.

Serves 4

For the roulade

40 g (1½ oz) butter
25 g (1 oz) plain white flour
150 ml (5 fl oz) milk
225 g (8 oz) broccoli
    florets

3 eggs, separated
50 g (2 oz) fresh Parmesan,
    grated
Salt and freshly ground black
    pepper

For the filling

2 red peppers
6–8 cloves garlic, unpeeled
½ teaspoon fresh thyme

1 teaspoon white wine
    vinegar
3 tablespoons olive oil

Fresh Parmesan shavings to
garnish

To make the roulade, melt the butter, then stir in the flour and cook for 2 minutes. Pour on the milk and, stirring continuously, bring to the boil. Simmer for 2–3 minutes. Leave to cool.

Steam the broccoli florets until tender, then chop finely.

Add the egg yolks to the white sauce, then add the broccoli and Parmesan and season well. Whisk the egg whites until stiff and fold in.

Pre-heat the oven to 200°C/400°F/gas 6 and line a Swiss roll tin with baking parchment and spoon in the roulade mixture. Bake for 12–15 minutes or until just firm. Leave to cool. Cover with a damp tea-towel to prevent the roulade from drying out.

To make the filling, roast the peppers whole for 30–40 minutes at 200°C/400°F/gas 6 or until the skins are charred. Leave to cool and peel. Roast the garlic cloves for 10 minutes, then peel.

Blend the peppers with the garlic and the remaining ingredients until smooth. Season to taste. Spread the filling over the roulade and roll up. Garnish with Parmesan shavings.

Bruschetta

Soft breads made with olive oil are ideal for making bruschetta. Use the *Sun-dried Tomato Bread* (page 195), *Olive and Walnut Ring* (page 192), or *Cheese and Sesame Focaccia* (page 187, omitting the cheese). Otherwise buy a plain focaccia or ciabatta. I've given a couple of simple ideas for toppings. You can add basil leaves, olive paste, or roasted peppers to make numerous different toasts. Serve them hot as a snack or as part of a light lunch.

SERVES 8–10

Enough bread for 6–8 slices   *Cloves of garlic, peeled and*
Olive oil   *cut in half*

For the sun-dried tomato topping

3–4 sun-dried tomatoes (in oil),   *Freshly grated Parmesan or*
cut in strips   *pecorino cheese*

For the pesto topping

2–3 teaspoons pesto
Slices of fresh tomato
50 g (2 oz) soft goat's cheese

Pre-heat the oven to 200°C/400°F/gas 6.

Slice the bread and bake for 5–7 minutes, remove from the oven and brush with olive oil, then rub over the surface with a cut clove of garlic.

Place the sun-dried tomato strips on some of the slices, then cover with grated cheese. Put the slices back in the oven until the cheese has melted.

Spread the pesto over the remaining bread slices, then cover with a slice of fresh tomato and a slice of goat's cheese. Put back in the oven until the cheese has just melted. Serve immediately.

Croûtons and Crudités
with Almond Mayonnaise

Whilst grilled vegetables and roasted vegetables have taken priority over plain raw vegetables, I think there is still a place for serving crudités at a buffet. The fresh crisp flavours balance the more oil-laden dressings.

Crudités in themselves can end up being a little dull so I think it is good to serve some flavoured croûtons amongst the vegetables. You can vary the spices and herbs used as you like.

Instead of the Almond Mayonnaise you could serve them with *Salsa Verde* (page 24), *Piquant Tomato Sauce* (page 215) or *Soured Cream and Chive Dip* (page 223).

OVERLEAF
Left: *Ratatouille Vinaigrette* (page 204)
Right: *Bruschetta* with sun-dried tomato
and pesto toppings

SERVES 4

For the croûtons

2–3 thick slices wholemeal
 or white bread
3 tablespoons walnut
 or hazelnut oil
Salt and freshly ground black
 pepper

½ teaspoon paprika
 or 1 tablespoon chopped
 fresh herbs (such as parsley,
 thyme, rosemary)

For the almond mayonnaise

50 g (2 oz) blanched almonds
A pinch of salt
85 ml (3 fl oz) water

2 tablespoons red wine
 vinegar
250 ml (8 fl oz) sunflower oil

For the crudités, choose from:

Carrots, peeled and cut into
 sticks
Sugar snap peas, trimmed
Cucumber, cut in sticks

Radishes, trimmed and left whole
Button mushrooms, wiped and
 halved
Spring onions, trimmed

Pre-heat the oven to 200°C/400°F/gas 6. Cut the bread into small cubes. Put the oil and seasoning in a small bowl and toss in the bread cubes. Bake these on a baking tray lined with baking parchment for 5 minutes or until quite crisp. Half-way through baking, sprinkle the croûtons with paprika or chopped herbs if you like. Leave to cool.

Toast the almonds at 200°C/400°F/gas 6 for 4–5 minutes, then grind to a fine powder with a pinch of salt. Add the water and red wine vinegar and blend again until very smooth. Then, keeping the processor or liquidizer running, add the sunflower oil a little at a time until the mixture has the consistency of mayonnaise. Thin if necessary with extra hot water or lemon juice.

Serve the vegetables and croûtons in separate groups on a platter with the mayonnaise in a small bowl.

Ratatouille Vinaigrette

This is quite different from a traditional ratatouille in that the vegetables are all roasted and then tossed into a herb vinaigrette. The cooked tomatoes blend with the dressing creating a sauce, whilst the roasted vegetables keep a crisp texture.

SERVES 4

4 tablespoons olive oil
Salt and freshly ground black
    pepper
350 g (12 oz) aubergine, cut into
    cubes
350 g (12 oz) courgettes, diced

1 red pepper deseeded and cut
    into strips
1 yellow pepper deseeded and
    cut into strips
225 g (8 oz) fresh plum tomatoes

For the dressing

4 tablespoons olive oil
2 tablespoons tarragon vinegar
1 clove garlic, peeled and
    crushed
½ teaspoon Dijon mustard

1 tablespoon chopped fresh
    tarragon
½ teaspoon sugar
Salt and freshly ground black
    pepper

Pre-heat the oven to 200°C/400°F/gas 6.

Put 2 tablespoons olive oil in a large bowl and season well. Toss the aubergine cubes in the seasoned oil, then spread out in a single layer on a baking sheet and roast for 15–20 minutes, turning the pieces once or twice. Add 2 more tablespoons of oil to the bowl, then toss in the courgettes and peppers. Spread these out on a baking sheet and roast for 15 minutes.

Cut the plum tomatoes in half lengthways and brush with any oil that remains in the bowl. Put on a baking sheet and roast for 15 minutes.

Mix the dressing ingredients together, season to taste and pour into the large bowl. Toss in the roasted aubergines, peppers and courgettes. Remove the skins from the tomatoes and chop roughly. Add to the vegetables. Adjust the seasoning and serve warm or at room temperature.

Roquefort and Rice with Roasted Walnuts

The strongly flavoured Roquefort pairs well with walnuts in this creamy rice dish. It can be made in advance and stored in the fridge, but allow time for it to come to room temperature before serving.

SERVES 6–8

225 g (8 oz) white basmati rice
100 g (4 oz) walnut pieces
100 g (4 oz) Roquefort
100 g (4 oz) crème fraîche
2 tablespoons chopped fresh
    tarragon

Salt and freshly ground black
    pepper
75 g (3 oz) mixed salad leaves
    (such as watercress,
    radicchio, lollo rosso) to
    garnish

Cook the rice in at least double its volume of boiling, lightly salted water. Drain well and rinse in hot water. Leave to cool.

Pre-heat the oven to 200°C/400°F/gas 6 and roast the walnuts on a baking tray for 4–5 minutes. Cool and then chop coarsely. Crumble the Roquefort.

Mix the cheese, walnuts, rice and crème fraîche together. Add the tarragon and season to taste. Oil a savarin mould or plain round bowl. Press in the rice and leave for several hours.

To serve turn the rice out onto a large flat plate. Knock the mould sharply so that the rice comes out. Serve garnished with salad leaves.

A MORE FORMAL SUMMER MEAL

Chilled Melon and Peach Soup
with Elderflowers
or
Summer Bean Soup
Caramelized Onion Tart
Roasted New Potatoes
with Herbs
French Bean Salad
with Sun-Dried Tomato Vinaigrette
Carrot Salad
with Orange and Pistachios
Iced Lemon Cream
with Greek Yoghurt
Layered Summer Cheesecake

This menu is full of summer flavours which I think work even on colder days. Start with a chilled fruit soup or a light hot soup made with broad beans. The main course is a classic onion tart, good warm or cold with roasted new potatoes and salads. Finish with a choice of dessert.

Chilled Melon and Peach Soup with Elderflowers

This soup has a clean cool tang, perfect as a summer starter. It is best served in small quantities.

SERVES 8

1 Galia melon
4 peaches
6 tablespoons elderflower cordial

300 ml (10 fl oz) single cream
Crushed ice to serve
Elderflower sprigs to decorate

Scoop out the melon flesh and peel and chop the peaches, reserving 8 slices for decoration. Blend melon and peaches with the elderflower cordial until completely smooth. Add the cream and blend again. Chill very well.

Serve with a little crushed ice in each bowl and decorate with a peach slice and fresh elderflower sprig.

Summer Bean Soup

Broad beans are a neglected vegetable although they have a lovely colour and good flavour. I think it is their thick skin which is their least attractive quality. This puréed soup solves that problem. For a finer texture, pass the soup through a sieve.

SERVES 6–8

750 g (1½ lb) broad beans, shelled weight
2 onions, chopped
2 cloves garlic, peeled and crushed
3 tablespoons sunflower oil
225 g (8 oz) potato, peeled and diced

600 ml (1 pint) milk
4 tablespoons chopped fresh parsley
Juice of 1 lemon
4 tablespoons chopped fresh mint
Salt and freshly ground black pepper

Cook the broad beans for 5–6 minutes in plenty of boiling water. Drain, reserving the liquid for stock.

Gently cook the onions and garlic in the oil, then add the potato and cook until the potato begins to soften. Add the cooked beans, milk, 600 ml (1 pint) reserved stock (make it up with water if you have not got 600 ml/1 pint) and parsley. Bring the soup to the boil and simmer for 30 minutes. Leave to cool then add the lemon juice and mint. Purée until completely smooth. Season to taste.

Caramelized Onion Tart

Soft onions with a melting texture make an excellent filling for a summer tart as they have a good flavour when warm or cold.

SERVES 6–8

1 quantity shortcrust pastry, see
page 117
750 g (1½ lb) onions, sliced in
rings
50 g (2 oz) butter
2 teaspoons soft brown sugar

½ teaspoon salt
4 eggs
250 ml (8 fl oz) single cream
100 g (4 oz) Emmental, grated
½ teaspoon freshly grated nutmeg
Freshly ground black pepper

Pre-heat the oven to 200°C/400°F/gas 6.

Make the pastry, roll out and line a 25 cm (10 inch) flan dish. Bake blind for 5 minutes.

Slice the onions and reserve 6 slices for garnish. Fry the onions in the butter with the sugar and salt. Cook until soft and golden brown.

Beat the eggs and mix in the cream, grated cheese and nutmeg. Season to taste.

Strain the onions, reserving any cooking juices. Arrange them on the bottom of the pastry case. Stir the onion juices into the egg mixture and pour over the onions. Arrange the reserved raw onion slices on top. Bake at 200°C/400°F/gas 6 for 35 minutes or until set. Before serving place the tart under a very hot grill and cook until the onion rings on the top are well browned.

Roasted New Potatoes with Herbs

SERVES 6–8

900 g–1.25 kg (2–2½ lb) new
potatoes
2 tablespoons olive oil or Herb
Oil (see page 80)
1–2 tablespoons fresh thyme
leaves or rosemary needles
Salt and freshly ground black
pepper

Pre-heat the oven to 200°C/400°F/gas 6. Scrub the new potatoes then toss them in the oil, fresh herbs and seasoning until lightly coated. Place the potatoes on a baking sheet and bake for 35–40 minutes. Serve warm or at room temperature.

French Bean Salad with Sun-dried Tomato Vinaigrette

This salad is strong both in terms of colour and flavour.

SERVES 4

For the vinaigrette

50 g (2 oz) sun-dried tomatoes (in oil)
2 tablespoons red wine vinegar
6 tablespoons olive oil

½ teaspoon French mustard
1 teaspoon honey
1 tablespoon lemon juice
Salt and freshly ground black pepper

For the salad

450 g (1 lb) French beans, trimmed and blanched for 3–4 minutes
50 g (2 oz) pitted black olives
225 g (8 oz) tomatoes, quartered
100 g (4 oz) mixed green salad leaves

For the vinaigrette, blend the tomatoes in a blender or nut mill to a thick paste. Add all the remaining ingredients and process until well mixed. Season well. The vinaigrette should have a grainy texture.

For the salad, mix the French beans, olives and tomatoes and toss in the vinaigrette.

Line a bowl with the salad leaves and loosely pile in the salad.

OVERLEAF
Left: *Carrot Salad with Orange and Pistachios* (page 212)
Right: *Broccoli and Parmesan Roulade with Red Pepper Cream* (page 199)

Carrot Salad with Orange and Pistachios

SERVES 4–6

For the dressing

Juice and zest of 1 orange
3 tablespoons sunflower
oil

1 tablespoon honey
Salt and freshly ground black
pepper

450 g (1 lb) carrots, peeled and
finely grated
50 g (2 oz) unsalted pistachios

For the dressing, mix all the ingredients together and season well. Mix the grated carrots into the dressing.

Lightly fry the pistachios in a dry frying-pan until just toasted. Toss in a little salt, then chop coarsely. Just before serving, mix into the carrot salad, leaving a few to garnish.

Iced Lemon Cream with Greek Yoghurt

This ice-cream is for lemon lovers. The lemon curd has a sharp tang which I think combines well with the clean flavour of yoghurt. Do use a full-fat yoghurt for a creamy effect once frozen.

SERVES 8

3 egg yolks
75 g (3 oz) caster sugar
120 ml (4 fl oz) lemon juice

Zest of 2 lemons
450 ml (15 fl oz) Greek-style
natural yoghurt

Beat the egg yolks and strain through a fine sieve. Beat in the sugar, lemon juice and zest. Heat the mixture gently until it thickens and begins to coat the back of the spoon.

Leave to cool, then beat in the yoghurt. Sweeten with extra sugar if necessary although it is better if the flavour is quite sharp as this works well when the yoghurt is frozen.

Churn and freeze for 20 minutes. Defrost a little before serving. If making this without a machine, see page 173.

Layered Summer Cheesecake

Ricotta and mascarpone combine to make a smooth, snow-white topping for this light sponge. I find conventional cheesecakes have become rather sickly. This version is sweet and creamy but with a fresh clean taste. For the fruit choose any of the soft summer ones that are plentiful, like strawberries, raspberries or red or black currants. I use the Finnish liqueur Lingonberry but any fruit liqueur will do.

SERVES 8

For the sponge

2 eggs
65 g (2½ oz)213 caster sugar
50 g (2 oz) plain white flour

For the topping

225 g (8 oz) ricotta
225 g (8 oz) mascarpone
50 g (2 oz) icing sugar
¼ teaspoon vanilla essence

25 g (1 oz) caster sugar
3–4 tablespoons fresh fruit juice
2–3 tablespoons liqueur
350 g (12 oz) soft fruit

Pre-heat the oven to 190°C/375°F/gas 5.

Whisk the eggs and sugar until very thick. Fold in half the flour, then fold in the remainder. Spoon the mixture into a greased and lined 18 cm (7 inch) tin. Bake for 15–20 minutes or until beginning to shrink from the sides of the tin. Remove from the tin and leave to cool.

For the topping, mix the ricotta and mascarpone with the icing sugar and vanilla.

In a saucepan dissolve the caster sugar in the fruit juice and bring to the boil to make a syrup. Remove from the heat and add the liqueur. Split the sponge in half and soak in the fruit syrup. Leave for an hour or so. Sandwich together with a small layer of the cheese filling. Pile the rest of the filling on top. Just before serving, cover completely with fruit.

BARBECUES

Apart from organizing the weather, barbecue cookery should be a foolproof affair. If you haven't a brick built one, make sure the barbecue is placed on level ground. Charcoal is the best fuel. The time to start cooking is when it is glowing very hot and no longer smoking or flaming. Remember to have oven gloves rather than an oven cloth which may trail in the embers. Special long handled cooking utensils are available too though you can use ordinary ones with care. A pair of tongs is useful for turning the food over. If the rain suddenly makes you alter your plans, transfer the food to the oven and roast or fry. Grilling does work but it can be quite tricky to prevent the food scorching.

Fresh vegetables and fruits, lightly cooked over charcoal and served with a dip, dressing and good bread, make a colourful, easy meal. There are notes in this chapter to show you how to prepare these. The one disadvantage is that cooking the vegetables (and you need plenty) in a single layer, takes up a fair amount of space, so make sure you have extra resources of fuel to keep the charcoals aglow.

I've also included some recipes for savouries to augment a barbecue meal. There are two favourites, nut burgers and tofu kebabs, plus a fresh discovery – barbecued haloumi cheese which is well worth a try.

Apart from the savoury food, I've also included a recipe for sweet brochettes to finish off the meal.

214

Barbecued Aubergine Slices with Piquant Tomato Sauce

I think aubergines are robust enough to be included with main course savouries. I like to spread the cooked slices with a little of the tomato sauce and just serve them as finger food. For a more substantial dish, serve them with bread.

SERVES 4

1–2 aubergines
Olive oil
Salt and freshly ground black
pepper

For the sauce

225 g (8 oz) ripe tomatoes
1 tablespoon balsamic vinegar
½ teaspoon capers
3 sun-dried tomatoes (in oil),
chopped

1 tablespoon olive oil
Salt and freshly ground black
pepper

Trim and thinly slice the aubergine. Mix the olive oil with some salt and pepper and brush the slices well with it. Grill on a barbecue until well cooked. Turn the slices over during cooking.

For the sauce, pour boiling water over the tomatoes. Leave for several minutes, then drain. Peel and chop roughly, removing the seeds.

Place all the sauce ingredients, except the oil and seasoning, in a blender and process the mixture until smooth. Then add the oil and process again until the sauce is quite creamy. Season to taste. Serve spread thinly over the cooked aubergine slices, or use as a dipping sauce.

Haloumi Cheese Brochettes with Hot Pineapple

Haloumi is a great cheese to barbecue as it doesn't run and drip off the skewer. It develops a good flavour and pairs well with the sweet hot pineapple.

SERVES 4

For the marinade

85 ml (3 fl oz) olive oil
1 tablespoon cider vinegar
3 tablespoons chopped fresh
   mint

1 clove garlic, peeled and
   crushed
Salt and freshly ground black
   pepper

225 g (8 oz) haloumi cheese
4–5 slices fresh pineapple
2 small red onions

Prepare the marinade by mixing all the ingredients together and season to taste.

Cube the cheese and fresh pineapple, aim to get about 32 pieces. Peel the onions, but do not chop off the base. Cut each onion into eight, leaving each piece with a little of the root on so that the layers of onion hold together. Put the cheese, pineapple and onion in the marinade and leave for at least 2 hours.

Thread skewers with alternate pieces of cheese and pineapple starting and finishing with red onion. Barbecue for a few minutes, turning until the cheese and pineapple are hot and slightly coloured.

Marinated Tofu
and Vegetable Kebabs

The firm texture of tofu makes it ideal for threading on to kebab skewers. As tofu has virtually no flavour it is important to marinate it first. I've suggested a sweet and sharp mixture, well flavoured with garlic and ginger. You could also use the marinade in the *Marinated Tofu with Sesame Salad* on page 89. It helps if the vegetables are marinated too. The kebabs should be brushed with oil to keep the ingredients moist as they cook.

SERVES 4

For the marinade

Juice of 1 lemon
2 tablespoons dry sherry
2 tablespoons shoyu
2 tablespoons concentrated
   apple juice
2 cloves garlic, peeled and
   crushed

1 × 2.5 cm (1 inch) piece root
   ginger, peeled and grated
Salt and freshly ground black
   pepper

1 packet firm tofu
Selection of vegetables such as
 cherry tomatoes, button
 mushrooms, peppers,
 courgettes
Olive or sesame oil

Mix the ingredients for the marinade together. Cut the tofu into bite-sized cubes and place in a large bowl with a selection of prepared vegetables. (Cherry tomatoes and button mushrooms should be left whole, peppers and courgettes cut into suitable sized pieces.) Pour over the marinade and leave for several hours. Drain the tofu and vegetables then thread onto kebab skewers starting off with a mushroom.

Season the olive or sesame oil and brush the kebabs well with it. Barbecue for a few minutes, turning several times during cooking. The vegetables should be still crisp, and the tofu heated through.

Mushroom and Herb Burgers

This classic recipe works very well when barbecued. These fragrant
burgers are good to eat with a selection of grilled vegetables and dips,
and make a good contrast to kebabs. I like serving them with the simple
Roasted Tomato and Chilli Coulis on page 220.

SERVES 4

1 tablespoon oil
1 onion, chopped
1 clove garlic, peeled and crushed
100 g (4 oz) shitake mushrooms,
 diced
175 g (6 oz) shelled hazelnuts
 and walnuts

50 g (2 oz) breadcrumbs
2–3 tablespoons mixed chopped
 fresh coriander and parsley
1 egg
Salt and freshly ground black
 pepper

Heat the oil and gently fry the onion until soft, then add the garlic and mushrooms and cook until well softened.

Pre-heat the oven to 200°C/400°F/gas 6 and roast the hazelnuts and walnuts on a baking tray for 3–4 minutes. Remove the skins from the hazelnuts and grind both nuts finely. Add the breadcrumbs, herbs and cooked mushroom mixture, then add the egg. The mixture should be moist but still hold together. Season well. Leave to chill for several hours.

Shape into burgers and barbecue for 4–5 minutes on each side.

Roasted Tomato and Chilli Coulis

Prepare this simple coulis in advance, either using the oven or
barbecuing the tomatoes and chilli. Don't worry if the end result seems
watery, it needs to be or the flavours would be too powerful.

SERVES 4

4 medium tomatoes   *Salt*
1 fresh green chilli   *1 tablespoon chopped fresh*
2 spring onions, chopped   *coriander*

Pre-heat the oven to 200°C/400°F/ gas 6.

Roast the tomatoes on a baking tray until the skin bursts and slightly chars. This takes
5–8 minutes. Leave to cool, then peel and remove the seeds.

Roast the chilli at the same time for 15 minutes. Leave to cool, then remove the skin
and seeds.

Place the tomatoes with the chilli, spring onions and salt in a blender and process until
smooth. Adjust the seasoning. Just before serving, sprinkle over the fresh coriander.

Barbecued Vegetables

Choose a selection of vegetables which will contrast in both colour and texture. Toss
the prepared vegetables in a well-seasoned oil. Olive oil is excellent or use a *Herb* or
Chilli Oil (see page 80).

Cook the vegetables, turning once or twice during cooking. It is best to barbecue the
vegetables in mixed batches as they do take up a fair amount of space and while you're
waiting for the next batch to be ready at least everyone will have a bit of everything to
tuck into.

Once the vegetables are cooked drizzle over an appropriate dressing. I've suggested a
couple of easy recipes on pages 221–2.

PREVIOUS PAGES
Left: *Barbecued Aubergine Slices
with Piquant Tomato Sauce* (page 215)
Right: *Haloumi Cheese Brochettes
with Hot Pineapple* (page 215)

Grilled vegetables can also be served with a scattering of freshly chopped herbs, a spoonful of red or green pesto, or one of the fresh chutneys on pages 168–9. Sweeter vegetables also work well sprinkled with a few drops of balsamic vinegar.

Here's how to prepare a variety of vegetables for the barbecue:

Baby sweetcorn: trim and leave whole.
Button mushrooms and open-cup: wipe and leave whole.
Courgettes: trim and cut into ovals by making long diagonal cuts. (Small young courgettes and baby courgettes can be left whole or sliced in half.)
Celery: trim individual sticks and then split lengthwise.
Fennel: trim off the feathery tops and slice lengthwise thinly or leave in quarters.
Field mushrooms: wipe and trim the stalks. Leave whole.
Peppers (red, orange, yellow): remove the seeds, then cut into strips. The sweeter the pepper the better it is as the juices begin to caramelize as the pepper chars.
Red onions: trim any root leaving enough so that when you cut it into quarters or eighths the segments of onion do not fall apart.
Spring onions: trim and leave a portion of green stem.

Herb and Caper Dressing

The piquant capers in this dressing nicely balance out the oil.

MAKES 50–85 ml (2–3 fl oz)

½ teaspoon coarse mustard
4 tablespoons olive oil or
    flavoured oil (see pages 80–1)
4 tablespoons mixed chopped
    fresh herbs (such as
    marjoram, oregano, thyme,
    parsley)
1 tablespoon capers, chopped
Salt and freshly ground black
    pepper

Beat the mustard into the oil. Stir in the herbs and capers and season to taste.

Spoon or drizzle over roasted vegetables.

Rosemary and Fresh Ginger Vinaigrette

Ginger, hot and sharp, adds a lively bite to this dressing.

MAKES 3–4 fl oz

6 tablespoons olive oil
½ teaspoon finely grated fresh
 ginger
1 teaspoon fresh rosemary,
 chopped

1 clove garlic, peeled and crushed
2 tablespoons cider vinegar
Salt and freshly ground black
 pepper

Pour the olive oil into a clean jar or bottle, then add all the other ingredients. Shake well and season to taste. Leave for at least 24 hours before using so that the flavours infuse.

Spoon or drizzle over roasted vegetables.

Barbecued Fruit

Barbecued fruit is good served with either the savoury part of the meal or the sweet. Once cooked as a savoury, fruits can also be sprinkled with a balsamic or fruit vinegar. Serve them on their own, mixed with vegetables or with a lightly barbecued whole goat's cheese. Savoury fruits are also delicious with dips made from crème fraîche, fromage frais and soured cream. (I've given a simple idea on the next page and also included one sweet idea for serving barbecued fruit as a pudding.)

Select fruits for barbecuing from the following:

Apricots, nectarines, peaches: cut in half and remove the stone.
Pineapple: cut into slices, removing the eyes, and core if necessary.
Bananas: peel and cut into chunks.

Prior to cooking, fruits can be brushed with honey and coarse mustard, or a mixture of oil, concentrated apple juice and lemon juice.

Place the fruit over the hot embers and cook until tender. The sweeter and riper the fruit the better as the natural sugars will caramelize as the fruit cooks.

Soured Cream and Chive Dip

MAKES 150 ml (5 fl oz)

150 ml (5 fl oz) soured cream
4 tablespoons snipped fresh
  chives

Salt and freshly ground black
  pepper

Mix the ingredients together, seasoning to taste.

Sweet Fruit Brochettes
with Tofu and Maple Sauce

Choose the sweetest, ripest fruit you can as these will be even sweeter
once cooked.

SERVES 4

For the brochettes

A selection of fruit (such as
  apricots, nectarines or
  peaches, pineapple and
  banana)

2 tablespoons clear honey
  or concentrated
  apple juice
1 tablespoon lemon juice

For the sauce

½ packet silken tofu
50 ml (2 fl oz) fresh orange juice
2 tablespoons maple syrup

2 tablespoons toasted flaked
  almonds to decorate

Prepare the fruit as on page 222 and cut into slices, chunks or cubes. Thread a selection onto each skewer. Mix the clear honey or apple juice with the lemon juice and brush the fruit with it.

To make the sauce, put all the ingredients in a blender or food processor and process until smooth. Adjust sweetening if necessary.

Barbecue the brochettes for a few minutes, turning so that the fruit cooks evenly. Serve hot with the sauce spooned over the top. Decorate with toasted flaked almonds.

CHRISTMAS AND FESTIVE FARE

Whilst for the most part I like casual meals, suppers rather than dinners, I do love a formal meal at Christmas. I like the preparations, the carefully laid table, and the time given in the day for sitting down to eat. Yes, you are right, part of this is a fantasy as with two small children, I'm lucky to get two minutes to sit down let alone two hours. Nevertheless, in this chapter I have planned two full menus for Christmas. These are to serve 6–8 people. For larger numbers, I would be inclined to make the *Warming Winter Feast*, a buffet menu on page 238, simply because it is an easier thing to organize.

As for the formal menus, both have a distinctive centrepiece which I think is vital to the character of the whole meal. The second menu has a dairy-free main course and an optional dairy-free salad which you can use as a first course.

For both menus I've suggested the same pudding – a light chocolate roulade filled with a chestnut and brandy cream – if you wish an alternative to (or addition to!) Christmas pudding, or indeed if you are not having this meal on Christmas day. For a dairy-free alternative, I would suggest the *Sweet Fruit Brochettes with Tofu and Maple Sauce* on page 223. (Grilled or plain, not barbecued.)

Given that it is midwinter and liable to be cold, I've suggested a warming buffet as a party menu. Spicy snacks to nibble on, followed by a pilaf, which is easy to cook in large quantities, and an accompanying hot vegetable dish.

To help with these menus I've given a preparation run-down so that you can see what and when to prepare in advance.

MENU 1

Mushroom and Madeira Consommé
Elderflower Sorbet
Smoked Cheese and Apple Brioche
with Cider Cream Sauce
Cranberry and Orange Compote
Roasted Roots
Brussels Sprouts with Almonds
Celeriac Purée

Bûche de Noël
Fresh Cream Truffles

This meal has a striking mixture of textures and colours, starting with a dark, clear mushroom soup followed by a snow-white sorbet recalling the flavours of summer. For a main course I've chosen a rich buttery brioche pastry filled with a smoked cheese and apple filling that has a subtle tang. Finish the meal with *Bûche de Noël* or a traditional Christmas Pudding, followed by *Fresh Cream Truffles*.

AT LEAST TWO DAYS BEFORE (OR LONGER):
● make the elderflower sorbet and freeze
● make the Cranberry and Orange Compote and store in jars

TWO DAYS BEFORE:
● make the Mushroom Stock and store in the fridge
● make the Fresh Cream Truffles and store in the fridge

THE DAY BEFORE:
● make the brioche dough and store in the fridge
● make the soup
● make the sauce and filling for the brioche and store in the fridge
● marinate the root vegetables
● make the sponge roll for the *Bûche de Noël*

ON THE DAY:

- assemble the brioche
- prepare all the accompanying vegetables as follows: trim the Brussels sprouts. Have ready some toasted flaked almonds to garnish when cooked. Prepare the celeriac by peeling and chopping. Cook in a little butter until soft then cover with water or white wine and poach until really tender. Purée with crème fraîche. Season well. Keep warm or re-heat in a microwave
- prepare the filling for *Bûche de Noël*, assemble and leave at room temperature
- remove sorbet from freezer at least 30 minutes before eating

Mushroom and Madeira Consommé

Dried mushrooms and Madeira are excellent together, yielding warm woody flavours. A home-made mushroom stock is best (see page 29).

SERVES 6–8

25 g (1 oz) dried mushrooms (ceps)
300 ml (10 fl oz) Madeira
2 tablespoons olive oil
100 g (4 oz) shallots
3 cloves garlic, peeled and crushed
100 g (4 oz) button mushrooms, finely sliced

1.2 litres (2 pints) Wild Mushroom Stock (see page 29)
2 bay leaves
3–4 tablespoons chopped fresh parsley
Salt and freshly ground black pepper

Rinse the dried mushrooms, then soak them in Madeira for 1–2 hours. Remove with a slotted spoon, draining well, then chop finely. Strain the Madeira through a coffee filter.

Heat the oil and sweat the shallots and garlic for 10 minutes. Add the fresh and the dried mushrooms and cook for another 10 minutes. Then add the stock, Madeira and bay leaves and bring to the boil. Simmer for 15 minutes. Add the parsley and season to taste.

Elderflower Sorbet

Snow-white, semi-sweet, with a reminder of summer, the clean fragrant taste of this sorbet is ideal as part of this rich meal.

SERVES 6–8

175 g (6 oz) white sugar
600 ml (1 pint) water
300 ml (10 fl oz) elderflower
 cordial
3 egg whites

Dissolve the sugar in the water over a low heat, then bring to the boil and simmer for 5 minutes. Leave to cool then stir in the elderflower cordial.

Lightly whisk the egg whites and fold into the elderflower syrup. Put the mixture in an ice-cream maker and churn and freeze for 30 minutes. Spoon into a container and place in the freezer.

If you have not got an ice-cream maker, freeze the elderflower syrup (before adding the egg whites) for 2–3 hours, then whisk thoroughly and freeze again. After a further 2 hours, whisk again. Beat the egg whites until stiff and fold into the mixture. Freeze for another hour, then whisk again and freeze.

Remove the sorbet from the freezer about 30 minutes before serving.

Smoked Cheese and Apple Brioche
with Cider Cream Sauce

All the elements of this dish need to be prepared well ahead of time, leaving just a matter of assembly prior to the final cooking.

SERVES 6

1 quantity Brioche dough
(see page 186)

For the sauce

25 g (1 oz) butter
1 onion, finely chopped
300 ml (10 fl oz) strong cider

150 ml (5 fl oz) double cream
Salt and freshly ground black
 pepper

For the filling

2 tablespoons olive oil
15 g (½ oz) butter
1 onion, chopped
2 cloves garlic, peeled and
    crushed
120 g (4½ oz) shitake
    mushrooms, diced
3 sticks celery, diced

1 large red pepper, de-seeded
    and diced
275 g (10 oz) cooking apple,
    peeled and diced
100–175 g (4–6 oz) oak-smoked
    Cheddar, finely chopped
Salt and freshly ground black
    pepper

To glaze

1 egg yolk
A pinch of salt

Chill the brioche dough.

For the sauce, melt the butter and gently cook the onion until soft. Pour over the cider and bring to the boil and cook for 5 minutes. In a separate pan, heat the cream and boil for 2 minutes. Mix a tablespoon of the cider mixture into the cream, then pour in the remainder and season well. Bring to the boil and reduce until fairly thick.

For the filling, heat the oil and melt the butter. Gently cook the onion and garlic until soft. Add the mushrooms, celery, pepper and apple and cook for 10 minutes until soft. Stir in the cheese and 4 tablespoons of cider cream sauce, then season well. Leave to cool.

Pre-heat the oven to 200°C/400°F/gas 6.

Remove the brioche dough from the fridge and roll it out into a large rectangle. Lay it on a baking sheet lined with parchment. Spoon the filling down the centre of the dough. Make diagonal cuts into the dough about 2.5 cm (1 in) apart on either side of the filling, out to the edge of the dough. Fold the cut strips over the top of the filling to create an interwoven effect. Leave to rise for about 1–1½ hours, then mix the egg yolk with the salt and use to brush the dough.

Bake the brioche for 20–25 minutes. Serve hot with the remaining sauce reheated if necessary.

Cranberry and Orange Compote

The bright colour of cranberry compote makes a marvellous addition to a festive table. Its tart flavour works well with rich foods. It is an extra worth making, especially as you can prepare it well in advance.

SERVES 6–8

SERVES 6–8

Zest of 1 orange
150 ml (5 fl oz) fresh orange juice
100 g (4 oz) white sugar

450 g (1 lb) fresh or frozen
* cranberries (defrosted if*
* frozen)*

Steep the orange zest in boiling water for a few minutes, then drain.

Put the orange juice and sugar in a large pan and heat gently until the sugar has dissolved. Bring to the boil and reduce for 3 minutes. Then add the orange zest and cranberries and cover with a lid. Boil the mixture until all the cranberries have popped. Remove from the heat before taking off the lid. At this stage the mixture will be quite liquid, though it will gel more on cooling. If you prefer a thicker mixture simply reduce further by fast boiling with the lid on. Take care that the compote does not catch.

Leave to cool. Store in the fridge for up to four weeks. Serve cold.

Roasted Roots

These root vegetables have a subtle spicy undertone. Their finished
texture is softer than that of traditional roasted vegetables.

SERVES 8

For the marinade

300 ml (10 fl oz) olive oil
150 ml (5 fl oz) white wine
2 tablespoons chopped fresh
* parsley*
1 teaspoon cumin seeds

1 teaspoon fresh thyme,
* chopped*
12 whole cloves garlic, peeled
Salt and freshly ground black
* pepper*

24 shallots, peeled
4–6 medium parsnips, peeled
* and sliced lengthways*
4–6 medium carrots, peeled and
* sliced lengthways*

Prepare the marinade by mixing all the ingredients together and season well.

Toss the prepared vegetables in the marinade and leave for several hours.

Pre-heat the oven to 200°C/400°F/gas 6. Spread the vegetables out on a baking tray in one layer. Pour over any remaining marinade and roast for 30–40 minutes or until the vegetables are tender. Baste occasionally during cooking.

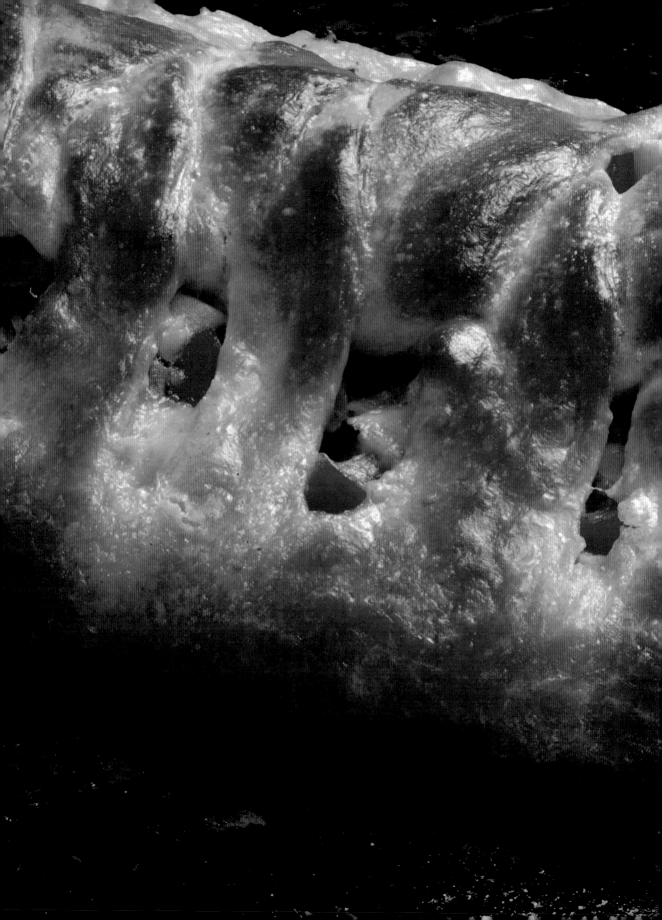

Bûche de Noël

This chocolate log makes a pretty festive dessert, a light alternative to a
traditional Christmas pud. I use dried chestnuts for the filling, but
vacuum-packed chestnuts are a good alternative.
A tinned chestnut purée is not so good as it is rather difficult to break
down to the right consistency.

I don't trim the ends of the roll as I like the uneven look, but tidy
them up if you wish.

SERVES 6–8

For the roll

4 eggs, separated
75 g (3 oz) light muscovado
  sugar
75 g (3 oz) plain chocolate
50 ml (2 fl oz) milk
75 g (3 oz) self-raising flour

For the filling

50 g (2 oz) dried chestnuts or
  100–175 g (4–6 oz)
  vacuum-packed chestnuts
2 tablespoons brandy
300 ml (10 fl oz) whipping cream
25 g (1 oz) white sugar
Icing sugar for dusting

Pre-heat the oven to 190°C/375°F/gas 5.

For the roll, whisk the egg yolks and sugar until light and frothy. Over a pan of hot
water melt the chocolate in a bowl with the milk, then leave to cool. Stir into the egg
mixture, then fold in the flour half at a time. Whisk the egg whites until stiff but not
dry, then fold in.

PREVIOUS PAGES
Smoked Cheese and Apple Brioche
with Cider Cream Sauce
(page 227)

Line a Swiss roll tin (28 × 36 cm/11 × 14 inches) with baking parchment, spoon in the chocolate mixture. Bake for 12–15 minutes or until just firm. Cover with a fresh piece of baking parchment and roll up. Leave to cool.

For the filling, soak the chestnuts for an hour or so (if using dried), then bring to the boil in their soaking water. Simmer for 35–40 minutes or until soft. Drain and cool. Grind the chestnuts (cooked or vacuum-packed) with the brandy until fairly smooth. In a separate bowl, whip the cream and sugar until stiff. Fold into the chestnut purée. Unroll the sponge and spread over the brandy and chestnut cream. Roll up and dust liberally with icing sugar.

Fresh Cream Truffles

Do use good-quality chocolate for these truffles. Once you have the basic mixture (cream, chocolate and butter) you can vary the flavourings by using different liqueurs, ground almonds or chopped maraschino cherries. The following recipe has orange flavourings. To serve the truffles, I think it is worth buying some proper paper cases as it makes for a professional finish.

MAKES 24 small truffles

200 g (7 oz) plain chocolate
50 ml (2 fl oz) double cream
50 g (2 oz) butter
2 tablespoons Grand Marnier
Zest of 1 orange

For the coating

Chocolate vermicelli or icing sugar

Break the chocolate into pieces and place in a bowl. Bring the cream to the boil and pour over the chocolate pieces. Put the bowl over a pan of boiling water and stir until the chocolate has melted. Off the heat, stir in the butter in small pieces until softened, then add the liqueur and orange zest. Chill until firm. Roll into small balls (this is very messy) and then freeze until firm. Roll each truffle in chocolate vermicelli or icing sugar. Store in the fridge.

MENU 2

Gruyère Soufflés
with Roasted Garlic Sauce
or
Roast Aubergine Salad
with Baby Spinach
(page 73)
Almond Strudel with Fennel
Savoury Apricot Compote
Roast Potatoes and Parsnips
Steamed Green Beans
with Tarragon Vinaigrette
Glazed Carrots

Bûche de Noël
(page 232)
Fresh Cream Truffles
(page 233)

Melting Gruyère soufflés start this festive meal which is full of flavours. For a main course, I've created a rich *Almond Strudel with Fennel* which goes well with a spiced apricot sauce. I've suggested *Steamed Green Beans with Tarragon Vinegar* as an interesting side vegetable, along with traditional *Roast Potatoes and Parsnips*. Roast these in a hot oven in sunflower oil or use a solid vegetable fat which I think gives a crisper finish. If you want the meal to be dairy-free, skip the soufflé and start with the *Roast Aubergine Salad with Baby Spinach* from page 73. Finish this meal with *Bûche de Noël*, or perhaps *Sweet Fruit Brochettes with Tofu and Maple Sauce* (see page 223).

TWO DAYS BEFORE:
- prepare the Savoury Apricot Compote
- make the Fresh Cream Truffles and store in the fridge

THE DAY BEFORE:
- make the sponge roll for Bûche de Noël
- make the filling for the Almond Strudel
- prepare the soufflés and sauce and store in the fridge separately

ON THE DAY:

- assemble the strudel
- assemble the soufflés with sauce to re-bake or prepare the aubergine salad
- prepare all the accompanying vegetables
- prepare the filling for Bûche de Noël, assemble and leave at room temperature

Gruyère Soufflés

Soufflés that are baked and re-heated work extremely well, especially for hectic parties as they can be prepared well in advance. You'll need to make some of the *Roasted Garlic Sauce* in the next recipe for this dish.

SERVES 6

300 ml (10 fl oz) milk
1 bay leaf
½ onion
A little freshly grated nutmeg
50 g (2 oz) butter
50 g (2 oz) plain white flour
100 g (4 oz) Gruyère, grated

4 eggs, separated
Salt and freshly ground black pepper
1 quantity Roasted Garlic Sauce (see below)
50 g (2 oz) grated Gruyère to garnish

For the soufflés, heat the milk with the bay leaf, onion and nutmeg until just warm. Leave to stand for 5 minutes. Strain. Melt the butter, then stir in the flour and cook for 1 minute. Add the milk, stirring constantly, and bring the sauce to the boil. Then cook for 2–3 minutes. Beat in the cheese and season well. Add the egg yolks.

Beat the egg whites until stiff, fold into the sauce. Pre-heat the oven to 200°C/400°F/gas 6. Grease 6 individual 200 ml (7 fl oz) pudding basins or equivalent. Fill them just over half full with the soufflé mixture. Bake for 15 minutes. Leave to cool completely then remove from the moulds. The soufflés can now be stored in the fridge until required.

Place the soufflés in a greased ovenproof dish. Cover with Roasted Garlic Sauce and sprinkle over the extra cheese. Bake at 200°C/400°F/gas 6 for 15 minutes, serve immediately.

Roasted Garlic Sauce

Don't panic at the sight of a dozen cloves of garlic. Once roasted, they have a wonderful subtle flavour and creamy consistency which works well in the flavoured white sauce. This sauce has a pouring consistency. It goes well with steamed vegetables or with the *Individual Celeriac and Goat's Cheese Timbales* (page 100) or *Celeriac and Emmental Strudel* (page 55).

MAKES 450 ml (15 fl oz)

12 cloves garlic, unpeeled
450 ml (15 fl oz) milk
½ onion studded with 6 cloves
2 bay leaves

25 g (1 oz) butter
20 g (¾ oz) plain white flour
Salt and freshly ground black
    pepper

Pre-heat the oven to 200°C/400°F/gas 6.

Roast the whole cloves of garlic for 10 minutes. Don't over-roast or they become diffi-cult to peel. Leave to cool, then peel.

Bring the milk, onion studded with cloves, and bay leaves to the boil. Turn off the heat and infuse for 30 minutes.

Melt the butter. Stir in the flour and cook for 2–3 minutes. Strain the milk into the roux and bring to the boil. Add the roasted garlic cloves and simmer for 5 minutes. Season to taste. Cool and purée. Heat through before serving.

Almond Strudel with Fennel

Moist vegetables and a mixture of ground and flaked almonds make a light filling for this savoury strudel.

SERVES 6–8

4 tablespoons sunflower oil
4 leeks, finely sliced
4 cloves garlic, peeled and
    crushed
450 g (1 lb) fennel, finely sliced
200 g (7 oz) ground almonds
300 ml (10 fl oz) cider

450 g (1 lb) cauliflower florets
50 g (2 oz) flaked almonds
Salt and freshly ground black
    pepper
8–12 sheets filo pastry
Oil or melted butter for brushing

Heat the oil and gently sweat the leeks and garlic until soft. Add the fennel and cook until tender. Stir in the ground almonds and cook for 1 minute, then add the cider and heat until thickened.

Steam the cauliflower florets for 5–8 minutes until tender. Mix into the almond and fennel mixture. Add the flaked almonds, then season to taste. Pre-heat the oven to 200°C/400°F/gas 6.

Oil an 20 × 28 cm (8 × 11 inch) oblong dish, cover with 1–1½ sheets of filo allowing some to come up the sides. Brush well with sunflower oil or melted butter, then repeat making three more layers. Spoon over the filling and cover with the remaining filo mak-ing four more layers brushing each with sunflower oil or melted butter. Tuck in the edges. Cut through the filo sheets to make a diagonal pattern.

Bake for 20 minutes or until the pastry is golden brown.

Savoury Apricot Compote

This useful sweet/savoury sauce goes well with the *Leek and Pecan Fritters with Fresh Sage* page 20 or *Mushroom and Herb Burgers* page 217. I think it more attractive if the shallots are left whole.

SERVES 6–8

2 tablespoons sunflower oil
225 g (8 oz) shallots, peeled and trimmed
½ teaspoon ground cinnamon
100 g (4 oz) dried apricots, soaked for 2 hours in water

350 ml (12 fl oz) passata (page 124)
Zest and juice of 1 orange
1 tablespoon red wine vinegar
Salt and freshly ground black pepper

Heat the oil and gently fry the shallots until just beginning to soften. Add the cinnamon and cook for a minute. Then add the drained soaked apricots, passata, orange zest and juice and red wine vinegar. Bring the liquid to the boil, then simmer for 40–45 minutes or until the apricots and shallots are tender. Season well.

Steamed Green Beans with Tarragon Vinaigrette

SERVES 6–8

For the vinaigrette

5 tablespoons olive oil
1 tablespoon tarragon vinegar
1 teaspoon concentrated apple juice
½ teaspoon Dijon mustard
Salt and freshly ground black pepper

900 g (2 lb) fine green beans, trimmed

Prepare the vinaigrette by mixing all the ingredients together. Season well.

Steam the green beans for 5–6 minutes or until just tender. Toss in the vinaigrette and serve immediately.

Glazed Carrots

SERVES 6–8

*750–900 g (1½–2 lb) carrots,
peeled and chopped
50 g (2 oz) butter
2 tablespoons white sugar*

Prepare the carrots and place in a pan. Add water so that the carrots are just covered. Add the butter in small pieces and sprinkle over the sugar.

Bring the carrots to the boil, and boil uncovered until the water has evaporated. Serve immediately.

A WARMING WINTER FEAST

*Spicy Spinach Rolls
Melting Cheese Parcels
(page 101)
Roasted Savoury Nuts
(page 239)*

*Party Pilaf
Puy Lentil Tajine
with Lemon and Ginger*

*New Year's Eve Chocolate Cake
Lime and Passion Fruit Pavlova
(page 176)*

The main part of this meal, the pilaf and the tajine, are easy dishes to prepare, will stand lengthy cooking and are therefore ideal for entertaining largish numbers with hot food. With the main course I would also serve the *Yoghurt with Cardamom and Pistachio* on page 167. For a more elaborate meal, it's a good idea to have some snacks and nibbles to hand round before the main course. I've suggested an unusual layered spinach snack. The miniature *Melting Cheese*

Parcels on page 101 are good too. *Roasted Savoury Nuts* are delicious and simple. Just toss the nuts (cashews are my favourite) in a little oil, spread in one layer, roast in a hot oven for 5–6 minutes, then toss in 1–2 tablespoons shoyu and roast for a minute or two longer. This also works well with almonds and sunflower seeds.

Depending on time and numbers, you could also serve *Mixed Vegetable Pakora* (page 157) or *Roasted Baby Sweetcorn with Rosemary* (page 20) and a selection of chutneys (pages 168–9).

THE DAY BEFORE:
- prepare the pilaf to the stage where the rice is cooked but the final ingredients have not been added
- prepare the tajine
- prepare the layered spinach but do not fry
- prepare the yoghurt
- roast the savoury nuts and store in an airtight jar

ON THE DAY:
- finish the pilaf
- finish the layered spinach
- heat the tajine
- prepare any other snacks

Spicy Spinach Rolls

These bite-sized rolls of spinach leaves are layered with a spiced batter and then cooked, cooled, sliced and then fried. The end result is a delicious and unusual snack.

Try to buy large spinach leaves which will be less fiddly to deal with. Don't worry if the rolls of leaves uncurl slightly or look rather sad at the end of steaming. The frying process is the key to finishing the whole thing off.

SERVES 8–10

For the batter

90 g (3½ oz) gram flour
1 tablespoon oil
A pinch of chilli powder
¼ teaspoon asafoetida (see page 59)

¼ teaspoon salt
¼ teaspoon sugar
85 ml (3 fl oz) water

24–30 spinach leaves (depending on their size)
Oil for frying

2 teaspoons sesame seeds
1 teaspoon black mustard seeds

To make the batter, mix the gram flour with the oil and all the spices, salt and sugar. Add enough water to make a batter that is slightly thicker than pancake batter (too thin to spread, too thick to run off the leaves).

Prepare the spinach leaves by washing well and drying. Spoon a little of the batter onto a spinach leaf and smooth it over evenly. Cover with another leaf and spoon over more batter. Repeat with 4 leaves, then roll the leaves into a cigar shaped roll. Repeat with the other leaves. Place the spinach rolls in a lightly greased steamer and cook for 40–45 minutes or until the batter looks set. Leave the rolls to cool.

When cool slice into rounds about 1 cm (½ inch) wide. Heat a small amount of oil in a large frying-pan, add the sesame and black mustard seeds and gently toast. Then add the spinach rounds (in batches if necessary) and fry until crisp and lightly browned. Serve warm, or at room temperature.

Party Pilaf

This is a Persian-style rice dish where the saffron-coloured grains are mixed with dried fruit and nuts. The rice is gently cooked in a large dish on the bottom of which is a mixture of rice, egg and yoghurt that makes a delicious crust.

It is an ideal rice dish for a party as it won't spoil if cooked for longer than planned. The crusty base or 'tahdeeg' can be served separately and eaten in pieces. Clarified butter, if you don't want to make it yourself, is available in supermarkets or Indian shops.

SERVES 8–10

450 g (1 lb) basmati rice	100 g (4 oz) currants
2 tablespoons salt	50–75 g (2–3 oz) dried apricots,
A large pinch of saffron	cut in fine slivers
1 egg	75 g (3 oz) slivered almonds
2 tablespoons thick natural	10 cardamom pods, seeds
yoghurt	crushed
Juice and zest of 2 lemons	2 tablespoons sunflower oil

To garnish
3–4 tablespoons clarified butter
(see above)
Very fine fried onion rings

Soak the basmati rice for 2 hours in a large bowl of cold water plus 1 tablespoon salt. Drain and rinse well. Grind the saffron in a pestle and mortar. Add 150 ml (5 fl oz) boiling water to make a saffron infusion.

Bring to the boil a large quantity of fresh water, add most of the saffron infusion reserving two tablespoons. Add the rice. Cook for 5 minutes. Drain.

Beat the egg with the yoghurt and 2 tablespoons saffron liquid. Spoon in 10 tablespoons of cooked rice. Mix the remaining rice with the lemon juice and zest, currants, apricots, almonds and crushed cardamom seeds. Heat 2 tablespoons oil in a large lidded saucepan, cover with the egg rice mixture, then lightly sprinkle over the remaining rice.

Poke 3 holes in the rice to let out the steam. Put the lid on the pan and wrap a clean tea towel around it to absorb the steam. Cook over a low heat for 1 hour. This dish will cook for a good deal longer without spoiling.

When ready to serve pour over the clarified butter and garnish with onion rings. To serve, spoon out the rice, then serve the crust separately.

Puy Lentil Tajine with Lemon and Ginger

This colourful, moist mixture of braised vegetables and lentils in a fragrant sauce is a perfect accompaniment to the Persion rice in the previous recipe. The longer it cooks, the more muted the colours become but the flavours develop.

SERVES 8–10

225 g (8 oz) puy lentils
4 tablespoons sunflower oil
450 g (1 lb) onion, finely chopped
2 cloves garlic, peeled and crushed
1 teaspoon ground cinnamon
2 teaspoons ground coriander
½ teaspoon ground cardamom seeds
1 × 2.5 cm (1 in) piece root ginger, peeled and grated
1 lemon, cut in eighths
2 red peppers, de-seeded and cut into strips

2 yellow peppers, de-seeded and cut into strips
450 g (1 lb) fine green beans, trimmed and chopped
450 g (1 lb) courgettes, trimmed and cut into matchsticks
450 g (1 lb) carrots, trimmed and cut into matchsticks
450 g (1 lb) passata (see page 124)
Salt and freshly ground black pepper
3–4 tablespoons chopped fresh coriander or parsley

OVERLEAF
Left: *Party Pilaf* (page 240)
Right: *Puy Lentil Tajine with Lemon and Ginger*

Wash the lentils and soak them for 2–3 hours. Drain, rinse, then bring to the boil in fresh water and cook for 30–40 minutes or until soft. Drain, reserving the stock.

Heat the oil and gently fry the onion and garlic. Then add the spices and eighths of lemon and fry for 2–3 minutes. Next add all the vegetables, mix in well and cook over a very low heat for 10 minutes or until just beginning to soften. Add the passata and cooked lentils and bring the mixture to the boil. Simmer, covered, for 30–40 minutes. Add a little of the lentil stock if necessary. Season to taste. Serve hot, garnished with plenty of coriander or parsley.

New Year's Eve Chocolate Cake

My Austrian sister-in-law makes a version of this traditional chocolate cake for us every New Year's Eve to eat at midnight along with a glass of champagne. For more notes on chocolate see page 172.

SERVES 8–10

100 g (4 oz) butter
150 g (5 oz) light muscovado sugar
90 g (3½ oz) dark chocolate, melted over hot water

3 eggs, separated
100 ml (3½ fl oz) milk
150 g (5 oz) plain flour
1 teaspoon baking powder
2–3 tablespoons redcurrant or raspberry jam

For the icing

90 g (3½ oz) dark chocolate
50 g (2 oz) butter
3 tablespoons double cream
75 g (3 oz) icing sugar

Pre-heat the oven to 160°C/325°F/gas 3.

Grease and line an 18 cm (7 inch) deep cake tin. Cream the butter and the sugar together. Add the chocolate, then beat in the egg yolks. Stir in the milk and fold in the flour and baking powder. Whisk the egg whites and fold in. Spoon into prepared tin. Bake for 1 hour or until cooked. Leave to cool.

Split the cake and sandwich together with the jam.

To make the icing, melt the chocolate and the butter together in a bowl over hot water. Whisk in the cream and icing sugar and beat until smooth. Spread thinly over the top and sides.

SEASONAL MENUS

On the whole I think that most food goes with other foods, but that is too vague a starting point to be helpful. I've drawn together some ideas for menus which I hope will act as a starting point. I've given these menus a seasonal emphasis as I find I'm looking for different sorts of meals depending on the time of year. Also I've tried to take advantage of foods in season.

If you want help with meal planning for formal occasions, look at the festive fare chapter where I have given a preparation breakdown. Those examples may help you when putting together other menus.

Spring and Summer Menus

I've suggested a few menus that make the most of spring and summer ingredients.

The first two menus are extremely simple and meant for very quick suppers, hence the pudding suggestions of fresh fruit. The next four menus are more elaborate and suitable for entertaining. Finally there's a list of picnic food, or rather food that can be transported and works well eaten cold.

Baked Italian Tomatoes with Basil and Balsamic Vinegar (page 93)
Oyster Mushroom and Pine Kernel Sauté with Buttered Penne (page 127)
Herb and Leaf Salad with Herb Vinaigrette (page 68)
Fresh Fruit

Bruschetta (page 200)
Avocado and Melon Salad with Pesto and Walnut Dressing (page 87)
Spinach Linguine with Tomato, Dill and Parmesan Sauce (page 126)
Fresh Fruit

Sun-dried Tomato Bread (page 195)
Patty Pans, Baby Aubergines and Tomatoes in Goat's Cheese Sauce (page 49)
Fennel and Parmesan Risotto (page 146)
Wild Mushroom Ragout (page 28)
Melon and Strawberry Brochettes with Sabayon Sauce (page 177)

Salsa Verde with Grilled Vegetables (page 24)
Tian of Artichoke, Feta and Bulgar Wheat (page 110)
Stuffed Field Mushrooms with Red Pesto (page 35)
Orange Cheese with Passion Fruit and Orange Sauce (page 178)

Globe Artichokes with Roasted Hazelnut
Mayonnaise (page 85)
Courgette and Chervil Galette
with Lemon (page 12)
Roast Peppers with Walnut Vinaigrette
and Sorrel (page 74)
Glazed Carrots (page 238)
Chocolate and Cinnamon
Ice-cream (page 172)

Courgette and Green Olive
Soup (page 18)
Enriched White Plait with Egg
Glaze (page 188)
Baby Vegetables in Filo Shells
with Crème Fraîche (page 47)
New Potato Salad and Blue
Cheese Dressing (page 108)
Crisp Lettuce with Strawberry and
Mint Vinaigrette (page 69)
Bilberry Brûlée (page 171)

PICNIC FARE

Baby Vegetables Poached in Fresh
Herb Marinade (page 46)
Tortilla with Coriander and Parsley
(served cold in wedges) (page 16)
Cheese and Sesame Focaccia
(filled with salad) (page 187)
Warm Spinach and Roquefort
Quiche (page 117)
Aubergine Mousse with Crème Fraîche
(page 96)
Melting Cheese Parcels (page 101)
Almond and Pecan Baklava (page 170)
New Year's Eve Chocolate
Cake (page 224)

(see also the suggestions for a mezze on
pages 198–206)

Autumn and Winter Menus

This selection of foods is more robust and warming than the choice for spring and summer. I've suggested three full courses but if you're short of time miss out one of the courses or substitute the pudding with fresh fruit or a cheeseboard.

In the final two menus, I've grouped together some ideas on a theme, one Mexican and the other Indian.

*Butternut Squash Soup with Lime
and Ginger* (page 54)
Cheese and Caraway Scones (page 187)
*Vegetable Cacerolita with Cumin
and Walnuts* (page 166)
*Roasted Baby Sweetcorn with
Rosemary* (page 20)
Baked Potatoes
*Vanilla Pears with Caramel
Sauce* (page 183)

*Pear Soup with Cashel Blue and Paprika
Croûtons* (page 108)
*Chestnut Mushroom Gougère
with Pecorino* (page 34)
*Roasted Kohlrabi with
Almonds* (page 58)
*Chicory in Crème Fraîche with
Horseradish and Mustard* (page 69)
*Plum Crumble with Hazelnut
Topping* (page 180)

*Grilled Goat's Cheese with Oyster
Mushrooms and Radicchio* (page 37)
*Leek and Pecan Fritters with
Fresh Sage* (page 20)
*Jerusalem Artichokes with Cream and
Mustard Sauce* (page 57)
*Red Cabbage and Arame Sauté with
Orange and Sesame* (page 61)
*Sticky Pudding with Crème
Fraîche* (page 182)

*Spiced Beans with Chilli and
Cinnamon Salsa* (page 161)
Olive and Walnut Ring (page 192) *or
Seeded Cornbread* (page 194)
*Guacamole with Roasted Corn
and Peppers* (page 197)
*Quesadillas with Roasted
Tomatoes* (page 109)
*Dark Green Salad with Rough Tapenade
Dressing* (page 67)

Spiced Peanut Dhal (page 161)
Garlic and Coriander Nan (page 189)
Spiced Okra and Potato (page 59)
Pumpkin Korma (page 165)
*Minted Pilau with Peas and Pine
Kernels* (page 142)
Fresh Chutney (page 168)

RECIDE INDEX BY COURSE

248

INDEX

Page numbers in *italic* refer to illustrations